Atheistika

Matthew John Slick

ISBN:
ISBN-13: 978-0-692-18999-3

CONTENTS

ATHEISTIKA

Introduction

Atheistika has been an idea I've had for quite some time. I wondered what might happen if a society were purely atheistic, based on the principles of reduction of harm, moral relativism, and majority vote. Of course, as a Christian, I was slightly motivated to write this story in such a way that would make atheism look as bad as possible. But I avoided it. After all, some atheists can, for the most part, be as decent as Christians in behavior and motives. There is no need to demonize them as so many Christians do.

Recently on my radio show, a gentleman called up and asked why if atheism is so bad, that many countries in Europe which are mostly atheistic are doing so well with low crime rates and economic prosperity.

I explained that the Protestant Reformation has heavily influenced European countries and that principles derived from the Bible were woven into the culture, ethics, and economies. Though they have moved towards atheism, they still retain many of the principles found in the Protestant Reformation such as private property ownership, the right of self-protection, contractual fulfillment obligations, caring for other people, honesty, integrity, charities, etc. In other words, the atheist population is benefiting from its past Christian foundation.

Also, in those countries where atheism has been allowed to run rampant, there has been much death. Just think of communist Russia with Lenin and Stalin. Then there is Mao Tse Tung in China. Together atheist dominated governments have killed tens of millions of people in the 1900s alone. For more information on this read the article, "The Myth that Religion is the #1 Cause of War," found at https://carm.org/religion-cause-war.

For fun, I have woven into the story hidden things. Names are anagrams. Numbers have significance. Even left and right have meanings.

Finally, since I like to write short, succinct, to-the-point articles I carried that style into Atheistika. You will find occasional descriptive prose, but for the most part, it is intended to be lean writing, unlike my novel The Influence.

I hope you enjoy it.

Matt Slick

Chapter 1
The Island

Brian Slarone stood on the highest point of the island. The roughly160-square mile land mass had appeared abruptly about 32 years ago in the Pacific Ocean and had taken about five years to form. It was quick and seemed to stop as fast as it started. Geologists studied it and then abandoned it. At first, no one wanted the desolate, volcanic landmass. A few nations occasionally discussed among themselves who might claim ownership, but once Brian decided he wanted it, he moved quickly and using his influence, international connections, and incredible wealth, the Island was soon his.

Brian was the richest man in the world. He made his initial fortune in computer games. By the age of 18, he was already the head of a multimillion dollar company known as Invatisoft. His empire grew quickly, and his influence spread to several countries when his company's programmers were used to develop security systems for various corporations around the world. In overly simplistic terms, his genius in finding the right people for the job was aided by a particularly stellar ability to write programs that attacked his own software looking for security holes, which he would, of course, fix. He called it Counter Attack Technology, CAT for short and it was a secret technology he guarded with a passion. This edge is what undergirded his incredible success and astounding wealth.

The island was about 25 miles long, 8 miles wide, and had a varied, rocky topography with the highest point at about 800 feet. The volcanic action that brought it into existence was not yet finished, and the island slowly continued to grow towards the west, though at a much slower pace than at its formation.

Brian got to work quickly and hired a company to level out much of the rough areas and fill in gaps in the landscape. He also hired a dredging company to transfer ocean floor sediment onto The Island. That is what he called it, "The Island." He then imported dirt, a lot of dirt, from some landholdings in the United States to provide a foothold for foliage. Ecologists were outraged, but Brian restored those lands to their original appearance by replanting trees and brush. It was all done so quickly that there wasn't much anyone could do about it and, of course, lawsuits were something he could easily afford to endure.

Next came the wildlife. He hired biologists to develop a basic ecosystem of bugs, reptiles, amphibians, plants, animals, and birds. Within a few short years, a healthy bio-network was flourishing around The Island. All this was happening while construction interlinked The Island with paved roads, two huge solar-power stations, buried power lines, and strategically located residences for the workers who were busy around the clock converting the small landmass to whatever his imagination and money could produce. A desalination plant provided plenty of drinkable water, and with the regularity of the rains and a catchment system, freshwater became plentiful.

But no one knew what Brian was up to, and there were a lot of conjectures.

When asked, all he would say is, "I'm building something." This 'something' included thousands of homes, two hospitals, several movie theaters, ten schools, a small airport, two TV stations, three radio stations, a car lot filled with electric cars, grocery stores (not yet stocked), two golf courses, and everything else appropriate for a small city. Only, he specifically said no one was welcome to live there, aside from a few hundred temporary workers.

The Island became a curiosity to the world. Brian didn't mind the attention but largely ignored it since he was fixated on development which took about six years. Then, when it was completed, he ordered everyone to leave, except for a few hand-selected people who were necessary to keep the basic infrastructure working. So, there it was, an empty Island municipality in the middle of the ocean.

The news media had dubbed it The Ghost Island, a name Brian did not like. Theories abounded. Was it going to be a resort? Or was it his private playground for the rich? One of the theories that amused Brian the most was the Alien Residence Theory, ART, as it had come to be known among those who speculated that he was preparing for the arrival of extraterrestrials. No one knew for sure, and the media speculated more and more which was exactly what Brian wanted.

Finally, when the construction was finished, at a considerable and undisclosed cost, he called for a press conference and invited news agencies from all over the world to come to The Island and enjoy a few days of relaxation along with free room and board. Then, on a scheduled day, he would reveal the reason for his new creation. Everyone jumped at the opportunity and soon, news crews from around the world flocked to The Island.

Chapter 2
The Announcement

The meeting was held in the Slarone Center, a beautiful air-conditioned building that served as both a conference hall and entertainment venue. About 250 people from media outlets all over the world, along with their cameras, lights, equipment, and interpreters had all jockeyed for position in the Center. The place was a cacophony of movement where tech people wired and rewired endless streams of cables all leading outside to a glut of portable satellite dishes.

Their host was scheduled to appear at 6:16 PM, local time. When that exact minute arrived, the room was already quiet.

He slowly walked out from behind the curtain and gazed at the gathering as he meandered towards the podium which was set dead center, but forward, closer to the audience.

Brian was 6’ 2”, slender, and had dark features. At fifty years of age, he was in excellent shape. He jogged, worked out with weights, and was a vegetarian. He was on the good-looking side and possessed a developing head of salt and pepper hair.

Brian wore a jacket made of a beige colored material, with loose off-white pants and a soft, yellow shirt that buttoned up to the neck. His sandals reflected the casual atmosphere of the tropical island. It was an odd combination, but somehow it worked.

At the podium, he adjusted one or two microphones and then pulled out a single sheet of paper from his jacket. He didn't need glasses. A crinkling sound echoed throughout the entire room. Then, with a slow inhale and exhale, he spoke.

"I would like to say thank you all for coming. I know the trip is an inconvenience, but I trust that the amenities and the beauty of The Island have made up for it."

He scanned the audience. Everyone was watching closely.

"As you know, I have put a great deal of money into the development of what many of you have come to call Ghost Island, a term I hope you will abandon at the end of my announcement. Rumors have surfaced about the purpose of my undertaking here including such things as a resort, a military base, and even a landing site for aliens. Let me tell you that none of these are correct."

He reached for a bottle of water that was hiding inside the podium. After a sip, he continued.

"The reason I have built this island with all its structures, roads, hospitals, homes and such is so that people can move here and enjoy their lives. But, since I own this land and since I am a devout and outspoken atheist, I will only allow confessed atheists to move here. No one of any religious affiliation may obtain citizenship."

Immediately a low rumble crept across the room. Reporters scribbled notes and typed into laptops, further marring the silence. Hands shot up into the air.

"I won't accept any questions until after I am done. So, if you would be so kind as to wait."

They did.

He continued.

"I now officially announce that this island is a nation and is henceforth known as Atheistika."

More rumbles and typing.

Brian paused. He knew that it would take time for the reporters to process what he just said and after half a minute, a partial silence once again began to manifest.

Brian then reached into the podium and took out a remote control. He moved away from the microphones and turned his back to the reporters. With a small thrust of the hand, he clicked the remote, and a very large screen silently lowered from the ceiling. Once in place, a website flashed onto the huge white surface. On it, the following was boldly presented and slowly scrolled so everyone could read.

ATHEISTIKA.COM

When in the course of human evolution, it becomes necessary for people to free themselves from the bonds of ignorance and superstition we, the citizens of Atheistika seek to form a separate, permanent, and secular nation based on the principles of reason and the reduction of harm. We will appeal to science, facts, and evidence while abandoning religious dogmas and superstitious beliefs and thereby create a more perfect nation. Therefore,

We hold these Ten Truths to be self-evident, that…

1. The physical universe and what it contains is all that exists.
2. The human species is the product of evolution as is all life on our planet.
3. There is no god, no sin, no heaven, no hell, no day of judgment, no reincarnation.
4. Science and reason are the best means to learn about our physical realm and our species, and they should shape our beliefs and understanding about the world, ourselves, and our behavior.
5. All people are equal in value regardless of race, gender, or sexual orientation.
6. Morality is to be determined by both reason and the consensus of the population where we seek the betterment of humankind and reduction of overall harm.
7. Each individual is free to pursue whatever means by which personal happiness is increased, yet without harming others.
8. Each person is responsible for one's own actions and the choices made.
9. Healthcare and education should be free to all.
10. Religions and false ideologies have corrupted human thought and resulted in untold suffering and archaic morals. Religions should and will eventually be abolished in the world as science replaces superstition with truth and facts. Therefore, due to their inherent intolerance which

increases overall harm, no religious practices or gatherings are permitted on Atheistika.

These thirteen principles will govern the forthcoming population of Atheistika.

1. Citizenship is available only to those who agree to the Ten Truths.
2. All people born in Atheistika are granted the rights of citizenship who, at the age of 17, shall affirm the Ten Truths or their citizenship is revoked. Upon revocation such individuals have one year to leave the Island or obtain special permission to stay granted by the Representatives of their respective regions.
3. Should any citizen deny any of the Ten Truths he shall make his denial known. A Court of Decision shall then be convened, and the status of citizenship will be retained or revoked, depending on the nature and extent of the denial.
4. Atheist children of citizens who become god-believers are welcome to stay per the permission of parents or until such times as they become 17 years of age, the legal age of adulthood on Atheistika.
5. Atheistika's population will be divided into five regions: Central, North, East, South, and West. The Central region shall have two representatives. The North region shall have 3. The East shall have 4. The South shall

have 2. The West shall have 2. Each representative shall be elected by a majority vote, for a period of no more than two years when elections shall be held to reinstate or elect representatives. Each Regional Representative shall reside in the region that is represented by the office and shall not hold office for more than two consecutive terms.

6. Removal of a Regional Representative from office before the next election must be by a 51% or greater vote by the residents of that region or by a majority decision of the House of Egalitarian Law.
7. The House of Egalitarian Law shall be comprised of thirteen members elected by a majority vote from the citizens of Atheistika regardless of region. Disputes about legal issues of the 13 Regional Representatives as well as Laws concerning national issues are decided by the House. House terms are for six years and are subject to continuation per vote of the population of Atheistika, but are not to exceed two consecutive terms.
8. House Representatives may be removed from office by a 51% or greater vote by the residents of Atheistika with votes being taken on the first Monday of the yearly quarter. Upon the death of a House member, a general election must be held within 26 days to elect a new House Representative whose term length is to continue in place of the previous Representative's office.

9. Atheistika's government will be Democratic Socialist system overseen and detailed in its execution by the properly elected Representatives of the House of Egalitarian Law which will oversee the means of production and distribution of goods.
10. Private ownership of property, goods, and services is for citizens of Atheistika who are of legal age.
11. Atheistika will provide, via taxation, the funding for all services needed for the proper sustaining of the nation including natural resources, infrastructure, transportation, education, law enforcement, and healthcare.
12. Citizens will pay a 20% flat tax on all income and will be adjusted downward according to financial ability.
13. Atheistika will provide facilities of incarceration and rehabilitation for the reinstitution of a person's place into society. Should such a person or persons not comply with the established procedures for rehabilitation, provisions will be made, at the expense of Atheistika, for the transportation of said person or persons to a country of the person's choice, along with sufficient funds to maintain his life and liberty for a period not to exceed three months.

The scrolling stopped. Briian turned to face the media.

A strange calm hovered in the room. He scanned the faces waiting for the inevitable barrage of questions. But, people were surprisingly restrained. Some were tapping away on laptops, and others were whispering into phones as they worked to inform their people in their own countries, translating, interpreting, speculating.

Brian moved in front of the podium. “The entire text of this presentation is included in the brochures now being placed on the table at the back of the room. I am sure you all have questions. So, now is the time to begin asking them.”

Hands shot into the air.

“Yes,” said Brian as he pointed to a pretty blonde woman with a notepad. She stood up.

“Did you come up with these rules by yourself or did you have help?”

“They are not rules,” said Brian with a slightly elevated tone. “They are the truths upon which Atheistika and its laws will be built. And to answer your question, these are primarily my principles, but, yes, I did consult others on their wording and scope.”

She began another question, but he pointed to a man in a grey sports jacket a few rows behind her. He stood as the blonde sat.

“Mr. Slarone, do you really think that people will accept these truths as you call them in order to live here?”

“Yes, I do. I think there are enough educated and enlightened people in the world to fill Atheistika ten times over.”

A man stood up in front, without being called upon, and challenged Brian. "Why have any of these truths at all if you're an atheist? Why don't you just let everyone develop their own truths instead of abide under such oppressive control?"

Brian stared at him for a moment as he wet his lips and flexed his jaw muscles.

The room grew somewhat quiet.

"We are not barbarians," he said slowly. "Our behavior reflects our beliefs. If you believe in the judgmentalism and intolerance of religion, then that is how you will behave. But in atheism, everyone is equal, and tolerance is a natural result of equality. However, not everyone believes the same thing, not even among atheists. Some openly deny any god's existence and others simply lack belief. So, since I am what is considered a strong atheist and since Atheistika is my endeavor, I have decided that there needs to be some principles upon which our behavior and laws ought to be based. Of course, at first our laws will be general, but as time goes on, we will create a more specific set that reflects our unique and developing situation. I am confident that people are basically good at heart and that through reason and dialogue, a productive and prosperous society will be established that will eliminate poverty, inequality, and suffering."

Brian reached for the water and took a quick sip. His posture seemed to relax a bit.

A question came from the middle of the crowd. "If people are so good, why do we have so many wars and poverty?"

Brian dropped his head down just a bit and then raised it back up as if focusing. He gripped the podium again, this time a little tighter.

Another person shot out another question before Brian could respond. It was almost as though the reporters were sensing his irritation and were circling.

Another person blurted out, "What gives you the right to decide what is right and wrong?"

Brian held up his hand and waited for quiet to overtake the room. He paused, narrowed his eyes, and took a deep breath as he leaned forward. What came out seemed rehearsed.

"There is no sin no virtue, no God, no absolute right, and no absolute wrong. There is only cause and effect, decision and consequences. As a species we have evolved to become more enlightened than our dark-age precessors. All around the world people are freeing themselves from the religious slavery of myth and god-belief. They are shedding outdated morals. They are freeing themselves from the shackles of religious beliefs which have led to the death of millions. Therefore, we decide our own morals. We embrace the truths obtained by science. We develop morality based on evidence, reason, learning, and the reduction of harm. It is from these that we seek the betterment of all mankind which means we support everyone's right to live according to the dictates of their own conscience. Therefore, we atheists seek to increase the harmony, well-being, and prosperity of all people without the restrictive religious oppression, ignorance, or bigotry. We believe in equality for all, regardless of age, gender, sexual orientation, or the divisions of false social status. We are enlightened. We are atheists."

Each word in Brian's final sentence was accompanied by a single, pounding of his fist on the podium. When finished, the silence seemed to emphasize his declaration. He leaned back and adopted a slightly close-lipped smile.

Then as if on cue, a clutter of hands shot up into the air accompanied by a blur clamor of inaudible questions. But Brian didn't acknowledge them. Instead, he looked passed the people as he took a deep breath.

After a few seconds, someone shouted over the noise.

"How do you think the world will react to what you just said considering that the majority of people believe in God?"

Brian narrowed his eyes and exhaled slowly.

"Everyone is entitled to believe as they wish. If they want to believe in whatever god they choose, that is their business. But, here on Atheistika, we affirm atheism and will live without god-belief, without religion, without superstition. And accordingly, we will develop our own culture and laws and the world will see what unbridled freedom and enlightened thought can accomplish."

Some shouted out, "What laws?"

Brian jutted his chin forward and then backward.

"Everything is explained on the website, but to answer quickly, we will have the House of Egalitarian Law which will have that duty. Citizens of Atheistika will be able to vote on those laws, own private property, have the right to run businesses, make a profit, are entitled to free healthcare, education, and much more."

Someone blurted out, "What about guns? Can citizens own guns?"

"Absolutely not!" Brian threw the words into the room. "We are not barbarians."

The soft noise of the crowd was rising in strength and pitch but lessened slightly at his retort. A question rang out from the back. "And what is the population of Atheistika supposed to be?"

Brian opened his eyes wider and nodded once.

"About 20,000 inhabitants. I am also working on plans to extend the island over the next few years as its acreage continues to increase through its natural volcanic activity on the West side. Along with this growth, we will increase its population appropriately once the land is stable and developed."

Someone asked, "Why the name 'Atheistika'?"

"It reflects the true nature of the universe and the principles upon which this new nation will be founded."

A woman asked, "How do you know there is no God?"

Brian stopped at that question and raised his hands to quiet the room. This time it only lessened in intensity.

"I am only here to inform you of what this nation will be and what its foundations are. This is not the time or place to discuss the god concept since he or she or whatever you call it, has not been shown by science to exist. But for now, I point you to the website which has more information. It should answer most of your questions." Brian began to fold his notes.

"Does everyone have to speak English to join your Island?" asked a masculine voice from somewhere near the front.

"Atheistika, not Island."

Brian offered the correction quickly as he pointed at the crowd.

"A competent level of English is required. It will be the official language of Atheistika since that is one of the most common throughout the world and is the language of business and," with a slight chuckle he said, "it is the only language I speak."

"What commerce?" asked someone.

"Programming, Websites, internet security systems, just like Invatisoft. In fact, I hope to eventually move the entire company here."

The obvious ramifications to that last statement meant that a lot of people would lose their jobs around the world. More hands that shot into the air.

"Don't worry. We don't intend to have a significant reduction in our employees. There will still be satellite locations throughout the world. Most people will not lose their jobs."

More hands shot up as a few reporters competed to ask the next question.

"What currency will you have?" asked a woman loudly above the crowd.

"We will be seek to use crypto-currency coupled with an ID chip. But that is still in the works and won't be implemented for some time."

The room erupted into more questions as more and more people stood trying to gain the floor.

Brian held his left-hand up until the crowd grew silent. After a few moments, he looked at the cameras and narrowed his eyes.

"I invite all true atheists, all truly enlightened people, to look at the website atheistika.com and see what we have built. A virtual tour of the island is available along with the plans to develop our economy and import people. And, if you want to join this new nation and participate in a bold new life, there is a rather extensive questionnaire you can fill out. Of course, not everyone will be accepted since we only have a limited number of openings. But all the information you need is there. Thank you."

With that, he gathers his notes, ignored the barrage of questions, walked off the stage.

Chapter 3
The Influx

News agencies all over the world reported the meeting in a frenzy of commentaries, soundbites, and post-event discussions. The controversy that followed Atheistika was varied and constant. Many religious leaders denounced Brian for what they called a "poorly thought-out Island nation." Comedians seized the opportunity to poke fun at everything they could. Pundits both applauded and condemned him. Magazines and newspaper published articles and pictures. It was a free-for-all of attention both good and bad, and all it served Brian's plan very well.

The website was inundated with millions of page-views within the first few days. Brian hired a team of people to go through the requests and inquiries and look for the best candidates. They then did phone interviews and background checks. It took a while, but applications for residency were accepted, and the island had its first wave of enthusiastic hopefuls within two months. They were selected based on the Priority of Individuals. It was as follows.

1. Medical staff including doctors, dentists, nurses, etc.
2. Emergency response teams.

3. Plumbers, mechanics, carpenters, masons, builders, mechanics, electricians, etc.
4. Computer programmers, accountants, web developers, etc.
5. Teachers for all age groups and topics.
6. Service related industries such as restaurants, recreation facilities, etc.
7. General maintenance personnel for a variety of disciplines.
8. Farmers for the agricultural and animal industries.
9. Police enforcement.
10. Other individuals as needs arose.

The document was not meant to show the value of any person over another. Instead, it was a general guide by which the Office of Population Control could more efficiently guide the development of the island's greatest resource, its people.

The first four groups filled quickly. The rest, 5 through 10, took a bit longer. But, that was not a problem because the influx of people was controlled so that the island's resources and economy were not overwhelmed.

There were some glitches here and there, but that was to be expected. Within the first few months, new businesses surfaced to meet various needs. And, finally, after about two years Atheistika was filled to capacity, and was producing a Gross National Product of around 1.2 billion U.S. dollars with an average annual salary of more than $50,000. They used a combination of U.S. currency and cryptocurrency for logistical reasons, but were moving towards the latter.

When problems arose, the Regional Representatives dealt with them, but if there were some issues that required a more thorough examination, then it was sent to the House of Egalitarian Law. The process was surprisingly efficient.

Atheistika was a success.

Chapter 4
The Complications

At first, all the people on Atheistika cooperated and adapted well. Communities flourished, businesses grew, and new construction continued. There seemed to be a general feel of prosperity and hope. People enjoyed helping each other, solving problems, and demonstrating how the idea of an atheist nation could be a light and beacon of truth to the whole world. The standard of living was slowly increasing overall. In fact, as Atheistika's success became evident, more and more people wanted to move there. So much so, that a huge waiting list soon developed.

There were even groups of people that sought to imitate Atheistika's philosophy and practices in small communities around the world. Some failed due mainly to conflicts with laws in their respective countries, while others had a modicum of success but did not generate much interest or influence.

Atheism became a frequent topic of discussion all over the world. In fact, given the quick success of the new nation and its apparent prosperity, it became almost fashionable to be an atheist. So, worldwide, there was a huge surge in the number of people who identified themselves as atheists and "nons." Atheist churches started meeting on Sundays and many became evangelistic, emboldened by Atheistika's world fame, as they attacked religion and promoted science.

Atheist clubs and organizations multiplied in colleges, cities, and rural areas everywhere, except in Islam dominated countries where varying degrees of Sharia were in place and the consequence of being an atheist was severe.

Nevertheless, atheist literature became popular, and books extolling secularism and denouncing religious mythology and irrationality abounded. Hollywood even developed a sitcom about an atheist family and its dealings with irrational god-believing neighbors. In Europe, atheism, which was already well entrenched, enjoyed new respectability. Belief in God became less fashionable and even ridiculed.

As a result, Brian Slarone became one of the most recognizable persons on the planet, a figurehead of rationality and success. Documentary films were being made about him and, to Brian's disapproval, many people started to speak of him as a kind of secular messiah. He vehemently rejected that accolade and discouraged any focus on him. But, it didn't stop thousands upon thousands of people extolling his greatness and wisdom. In a Western European country, there even arose a group called the Slaronians who exegeted the Ten Truths far beyond what Brian considered to be their original intent. They became a political party that sought the conversion of all nations to purely secular entities based on the principles of secular humanism, evolution, naturalism, and of course, the Ten Truths. They published a track on social media that sayd, "All god-believers are not qualified to hold any political or leadership offices due to their irrational and superstitious ideologies that could only have a deleterious effect on society." Clashes between atheists and theists erupted here and there and seemed to increase in frequency.

Brian, of course, who did not approve of his surname being used as a philosophical movement, denounced the various forms of aggression. He said that religion needed to die a slow, natural death rather than be met with violence. But, aside from that, he kept out of the philosophical and religious frays as much as he could.

Unfortunately, with the emboldening of the atheists and the underlying derision of theism that was increasing in many countries, persecution grew. Those who believed in God were increasingly the targets of mockery, ridicule, and even sporadic, physical persecution. There were reports of people losing their jobs and their property being vandalized because they held "outdated and bigoted religious views." Though these were infrequent occurrences, they were steadily on the rise. This was a problem, of course, and some nations quickly moved to stop it. Pro-atheist groups began to unify, and there were rumors of more political parties forming in various countries based on Atheistika's principles. Some became aggressive while others did not.

Because things were happening so fast, Brian held a special conference in which he denounced any adoration given to him. He called for tolerance and condemned any persecution of those who believed in God or gods. He urged peace and patience. In fact, he even wrote an article condemning any persecution of theists while he promoted the need for love, tolerance, and mutual respect. He released it on Atheistika's website. It worked. Persecution subsided, though not entirely.

But, as with everything where people are involved, problems arise. It was no different on Atheistika. People owned private property on which they built or bought homes. Some rented. A few individuals became more financially successful than others, and they started to acquire additional businesses and properties. In one instance, a businessman bought and then tore down two neighboring homes to make room for his large estate. But, this blocked the ocean view of people living behind him. Grievances arose, and Atheistika's first lawsuit was filed.

Then there were accusations of unfair levels of taxation for the less financially successful. People complained about 25% of their income being confiscated by the government; it had already risen 5%. Others objected to road projects that damaged the environment, and accusations of lopsided medical care where more influential citizens were accused of getting better treatment than others. Those with the money were able to pay for more legal representation than those with less who often got the short end of the stick and they were becoming powerful. Resentment became more evident. Then, people began to take sides on various issues which meant polarization and conflict.

As a result, two political parties formed. They differed on such things as property rights, asset limits, fair and equitable distribution of wealth, the rights of production, proper representation under the law, and the level to which socialism was to be implemented. They became known simply by the rather bland titles of the Atheistic Socialist Party (ASP) and the Conservative Atheist Party (CAP). They had meetings, debates, and the more they talked, the more they separated and ridiculed each other's positions. In fact, there were several clashes in bars and a few arrests were made on both sides.

In spite of these glitches, the economy was stable. Businesses started, failed, succeeded, and adapted to meet various needs. But, because the population was small, when people lost their jobs due to business failures, it was felt more acutely across the general population. More people applied for welfare and this put a financial burden on the government which then proposed the increase of taxes by 1% - again. This was not received well.

As some peoples' livelihoods disappeared, a mild recession crept through what was becoming the lower income areas of Atheistika. This forced One Bank, which was government controlled, to foreclose on properties and gain assets. Complaints against the bank's strict monopoly and unyielding legality were becoming commonplace.

Graffiti appeared here and there with slogans like, "One Bank One God," and "One Bank Under Slarone," and "One Bank Takes All." Then reports of theft started to trickle in. At first, it was small things like bicycles, skateboards, and surfboards. But pretty soon there were instances of home invasions with the theft of expensive jewelry, cash, and electronics. This necessitated the increase of the police force from 23 people to 31 over a six-month period. It was blamed on the small recessions happening in some areas of The Island.

Then there were reports of hard drugs on The Island. No one knew how they got there, but the police were investigating a rumored smuggling operation. Prostitution surfaced as did an unofficial brothel. Alcohol became an increasingly common problem along with its resultant string of brawls that grew in proportion to the bars that opened. Though there really weren't that many, it was obvious that problems were increasing.

Brian was growing dismayed by all of this, but he knew that problems occurred in every society in one form or another. He accepted that it was the unfortunate reality of people coming together, even on Atheistika, though he was a little surprised at the level it of disturbances given the vetting process for citizenship. But, he knew that there would be those whose true character wouldn't manifest until it was tested. Some nondesirables would slip through the cracks, operate on the fringes of society, and, of course, did not truly represent Atheistika's Ten Truths. All things considered, it wasn't that bad. The majority of people enjoyed a pleasant and prosperous lifestyle.

But still, people were talking about how to improve things. At first, these discussions were sporadic and unorganized. Complaints rose about the slow means of legal address through the Regional Representatives and then to the House of Egalatarian Law. People wanted things to happen more quickly. The different political parties ASP and CAP each grew in membership and wanted a stronger voice in the formation and direction of new laws that would govern their nation. Their differences increased as did their rhetoric and anger. Both parties were concerned with the financial, social, and moral foundation of Atheistika, but their approaches were different.

The world was watching, and Atheistika's image began to suffer. Of course, Brian was very concerned and tried to encourage people to be patient. He would appear on local television and give reassuring, short speeches about how the legal system was working and problems were being addressed. His advice did a lot of good, but difficulties persisted. Eventually, another movement manifested with several thousand people from both parties who saw the need for unity and agreed to some basic principles so they could work together and bring grievances to light. They called themselves the Civil Rights Coalition (CRC). It was headed by a vocal, intelligent, and well-spoken woman from a European country. Her name was Shelie Grustof. She meant business.

The CRC wanted a meeting with Brian and the House of Egalitarian Law to discuss various grievances. They were persistent, and Brian finally, but reluctantly agreed. A meeting was scheduled.

Chapter 5
The Gathering

Much to the surprise of Brian as well as the members of the CRC, the Slarone Center was filled to capacity. There were two television cameras from the Atheistika Television Network (ATN), and almost everyone on the island nation was watching. And, to make things a little more interesting, several media outlets from the different countries had requested to be there. So, the whole world was, once again, viewing the proceedings.

The thirteen members of the House of Egalitarian Law, a group of four men and nine women, were present. Once the meeting began, Shelie approached the podium. A surprisingly strong applause filled the room. She positioned herself to speak and waited for the room to become quiet.

"I would like to thank everyone for attending and, of course, we all want to give special thanks to our great founder Brian Slarone. He has made all of this possible, and each one of us is exceedingly grateful to be here and enjoy this wonderful endeavor."

She looked over at him and nodded. Another round of strong applause erupted, though shorter lived. He nodded back with an appropriate and appreciative smile. When it became quiet again, she continued.

"We, the citizens of Atheistika realize that this new nation is experiencing its growing pains. A large segment of its citizenry has requested a hearing by which grievances can be listed and, hopefully, addressed by the House of Egalitarian Law in a more equitable and time-sensitive manner."

She looked at Brian again.

He smiled again with a feigned patriarchal approval.

"Our goal is not to add to the problems that are festering within our small nation. Instead, our goal is to seek equity and a commitment from the House of Egalitarian Law so that the grievances that we present will be heard and resolved quickly."

At that point, she nodded to a man who was sitting in the front row. He was tall, thin, expressionless, and dressed in a black suit. He had a briefcase resting on his lap. After the click of the locks, he opened it and pulled out a stack of papers. It was several hundred copies of a single, double-sided document. After closing the briefcase and putting it on the floor, he asked.

"May I approach?" They nodded collectively.

He walked to their table and handed a copy to each member. Then he handed one to Brian. He returned to his seat, and before he sat down, he handed the rest of the stack to the person next to him and nodded towards the assembly so they could be distributed.

Shelie continued.

"As you will see on our handout, we have a list of grievances and concerns. In keeping with the use of our technological advancements, we have developed a website listing our main grievances as well as those of lesser importance. It is located at the bottom of the handout. Those of you who are watching at home can check it out at your convenience. But for now, let me read some of the main issues that we at the CRC agree needs to be discussed and refined.

1. Expansion of private property rights with consideration of limitations on the devaluing of people's property as a result of building projects that obstruct scenic views.
2. An expedient means of legal recourse, with a Jury of our peers, by which disputes can be filed and settled with proper representation rather than by the vote of The Thirteen members of the House of Egalitarian Law.
3. Three-year term limits, instead of six, for the members of the House of Egalitarian Law.
4. One Bank's monopoly needs to be broken up to enable competition for the benefit of the citizenry.
5. Rights to Complete Privacy in our homes where citizens can do anything, anytime within the confines of their homes with the consent of other occupants and without harm to others, unless others wish to be harmed. We will elaborate on details later.
6. The right to protect ourselves in our homes with weapons if necessary due to the rise in crime.

7. Marriage in accordance with one's sexual orientation including considerations on establishing the minimum age of consent.
8. Abortion on demand.
9. Doctor-assisted suicide.
10. The complete freedom of speech in which we propose a place or places on the island where a free exchange of ideas can occur without any repercussions.
11. Recreational drug use and prostitution need to be addressed. They are presently operating in the shadows. They need to be legalized or made illegal.
12. Development of retirement funds and care for the elderly, funded by the State.
13. The environment needs to be protected, and an environmental committee needs to be assembled to oversee the natural resources on the island as they relate to further construction projects.

With the last sentence, she slowed her words and came to a stop. She looked at Brian. Most people then turned their attention to him as well.

He was still reviewing the document – with a slight, involuntary frown. The others murmured softly amongst themselves as they pondered the document.

Obviously, something had to be done.

Chapter 6
The Decisions

The assembly lasted about three hours. It was cordial, and even though there were a few people who became slightly agitated, overall, it was a good meeting. During the next week, Brian met with members of the House of Egalitarian Law as well as Shelie from the Civil Rights Coalition and everyone agreed to the following terms.

1. There would be televised nightly meetings on Monday, Tuesday, Wednesday, and Thursday where issues would be discussed and proposed solutions offered.
2. The population of Atheistika could view the proceedings on the local TV station and comment via a special webpage on their Internet if needed.
3. These comments would be tallied and presented to the committee during the meetings so that a more democratic set of decisions would be made.
4. If more deliberations were needed, the committee would table the topic, discuss it the next day, and present their findings afterward.
5. The final passage of new laws was up to the House of Egalitarian Law who would take the recommendations of the Decision

Committee very seriously.

The D&C, as the Decision Committee had come to be known, would consist of the seven of the thirteen members of the House of Egalitarian Law chosen at random, plus three from the Civil Rights Coalition, and the three selected from the five districts of Atheistika – chosen by popular vote from among those districts. The total was 13 so that a majority vote was possible.

However, Brian insisted that the process include a check system in the form of someone who would not vote on issues, but whose job would be to look for problems to whatever was proposed – within reason, of course. The goal was to expose unforeseen difficulties so they could be dealt with and thereby make prospective new laws that much better. It was reminiscent of the CAT (Counter Attack Technology) system that Brian developed in his company that sought out and identified potential, unforeseen flaws in security software programs. It worked for him then, why not now?

At first, the idea didn't seem practical because it would only slow down the solution process. But, eventually, everyone agreed. After all, it *was* something he suggested, and his opinion carried a lot of weight.

Brian insisted that the qualified person be well versed in logic, philosophy, and ethics. The legal aspects were, of course, the purview of The House of Egalitarian Law and would be decided by them. So, after searching through the ranks and qualifications of the population, three people were approached to play the contrary role. One declined and two accepted. Of those two, a man and a woman, the decision fell to a retired university professor, Dr. Gunter Challhert, who was from Florida. He was well educated and had taught philosophy and ethics for many years at a University.

Gunter was 53 and had a Ph.D. in Philosophy. He was about 5' 9", carried a slight pot belly, and had thinning dark and greyish hair. Round glasses matched his slightly round head, and he had a way of putting people at ease with his large smile and comfortable demeanor. He became what they soon dubbed as The Contrarian.

He and his wife, Martha, had moved to the Island within months of its founding and he had taken a part-time job as a professor at Atheistika's Slarone College.

And so, everything was in place, and the first meeting was just days away.

Chapter 7
The Contrarian

Gunter fumbled with his tie for the third, unsuccessful time. "I just can't get this knot right." He yanked, and it tightened into a slanted trapezoid.

Martha took control and positioned him by his shoulders as she began to correct the mess he had created. He acquiesced.

"I don't know about this Contrarian thing," he muttered.

"Oh?"

"I've sworn an oath to offer contrary opinions and to find better solutions. The first few issues raised are more governmental than philosophical, so I won't be saying much if anything. But, I'm concerned about the ethical issues dealing with self-protection, marriage, sexual orientation, abortion, suicide, etc. I'm afraid it might turn into a mess, and I am hoping people don't get mad at me for injecting philosophical counter arguments. But, I'll just be doing my job."

He was more thinking out loud than asking her anything.

With a final gentle tug on the tie, she was done. Then she patted him on both shoulders. "There."

He adjusted his glasses as he examined the tie in the mirror, then looked at her with just a slight trace of amazement. "How do you do that?"

"Practice."

He inspected the knot again and tried to adjust it, just a bit.

She gently slapped his hand away.

"Anyway," he continued. "The more I think about it, the more I wonder if I might have made a mistake. I'm going be arguing against our cause. It'll be like arguing against progress and change. Its going to make people mad." He turned away from the mirror and faced his wife. "And that's going to be a problem."

She locked one hip into position while she examined him. "What do you mean?"

He exhaled, walked over to a window, and gazed out into the sunlit landscape. Just beyond a small hill, he could see the blue ocean. He loved the water. It was calming.

"Generally, people don't like being challenged. They get attached to their philosophies. They build their worlds around them whether they are true or not. They don't think things through and, well, let's just say that cross-examining their philosophies often makes people angry."

He turned to his wife again and noticed how the outside light seemed almost to make her glow. She looked angelic. After all these years of marriage, his love for her had steadily grown. She was a good woman, and to this day he could never understand why she agreed to marry him. Though she had grown older, he thought she was more beautiful now than ever.

"You know something? I'll never understand what you saw in me. You're a good-looking woman, and you're smart. You could've married anyone."

She sighed with a well-rehearsed and feigned annoyance as she shook her head.

He added, "Of course, it was probably my incredible humility and abs that drew you to me."

She smiled. "I married you for all your money because all the good-looking men were taken."

"That makes sense." With that, he walked over to her and gave her a quick peck on the cheek. "You're lucky to have me," he uttered in a pretended arrogant tone.

"Yes, I am."

After a moment, he went back to the mirror, and with another feigned adjustment of the tie, he loosened it and lifted it over his head. Then he removed his jacket. "As usual, you have good taste in clothes."

"And men."

"Of course," he said with a smile and a cocked eyebrow. "This will look good tomorrow. Thanks."

She shook her head and let out a long exhale.

Gunter undressed the rest of the way, and after he hung everything up, he sat on the bed and stared at the floor. She sat down next to him.

"Tomorrow I'm going to have to do one of the most difficult things I've ever done. I'm going to argue against my own community's attempt to make itself better. That's weird. I'll have to try and find problems with their proposed solutions, and point out philosophical and ethical difficulties."

She placed her hand on his knee and said with a soft, reassuring tone, "You'll do great." Then with more annoyance, "You were always good at twisting words and making me want to throw dishes at you. So, tomorrow night will be a breeze for you."

He huffed out a quick, single chuckle. "Yeah, I've had a lot of practice annoying you over the years."

"That's for sure."

"I guess I'm pretty good at it."

Her face locked in an expression of acknowledgment as she slowly nodded.

He held her hand in his.

"I hope you're right. But I can see that there's going to be some problems if I do my job to the best of my ability."

He began to stare again into that distant place outside the window. After a full minute of contemplation, he finally spoke.

"Over the years I've taught many students. Most of them were complacent and apathetic. They just wanted to get grades in order to graduate and move on to something they cared about. But occasionally there would be students who would interact, who explored ideas, and some who would even raise some good objections. I always enjoyed that."

It took a bit to scrub the dust off of some memories before he could remember something more clearly.

"But there was this one student. He had a way of asking annoying questions. I mean, it was okay, but he kept pressing. He was polite enough. At first, I thought he was a religious nut, and I always considered that to be a detriment to logical and ethical thinking. After all, basing ethics on the arbitrary whims of mythical gods is, well, stupid. That is what I told him one day in class – but more gently, of course. He ignored my criticism with a smile. That smile made me angry and every now and then he would smile at something else I would say the same way. It was really annoying."

More dusting.

"He kept digging into the foundational reasons for everything, always questioning, always paying attention."

"What kind of questions did he ask?"

"Well, he always wanted justification for the grounding of rationality and ethics. He asked about what makes a belief valid and how do we know our assumptions about truth are true. He would question everything, and, believe it or not, when I applied his questions to his own god-belief, he accepted it and said he had no problems doing that. The conversations that followed were sometimes great and other times just dumb."

"In all my years of teaching, he was the one student who got under my skin."

"Did he fail the class?"

Gunter looked at her. "Heck no. I gave him an A. He was annoying but never rude. He was respectful, did his assignments, and he did exactly what I asked my students to do. So, I *had* to be objective and so I give him a good grade. He earned it, even though he contradicted a lot of what I said."

"But you know something," he said with a half-smile as he looked back out the window. "Of the years, sometimes I missed his challenges and annoying questioning. No other student did what he did and it was refreshing and engaging."

Gunter paused for a bit before he dismissed the memory. "The reason I'm bringing this up is because of what I'm supposed to do as The Contrarian. I'm supposed to question a lot of stuff. Of course, I won't be as inane as that student, but I'm worried that I may become as irritating as he was. I remember my annoyance with him – though I tried not to let it show. So, if I got upset with him in a philosophy class, how do you think people are going to react in the meeting when I do basically the same thing?"

His tone trailed off with a metered, contemplative timbre. He was examining his options, thinking through them and more or less considering what he needed to do.

He turned to her.

"So, the whole thing could devolve into an argument or something worse. I don't know what's going to happen."

"No one has all the answers to everything. Not even you," She replied.

"Oh come on, now you're just being mean."

She shook her head and stood up. "Hungry?"

"Yeah. Doing all this tie-tying makes me hungry. It is a lot of work."

She smiled again.

After a moment, he stared back out the window.

"I have always prided myself on finding answers to problems, well, philosophical ones, anyway. Now, I'll be finding problems with our nation's attempt to find political and social solutions."

He took yet another contemplative pause which his wife again patiently endured.

"Anyway, since I swore to do my job to the best of my ability, I'm *supposed* to be a little bit annoying."

With that she patted him on the knee and said, "I'll fix dinner." She stood up. "We can talk more later if you want."

"I guess I'm just processing it all, thinking it through." After another exhale, he said, "Thanks for listening."

"You'll do fine."

He stood up. "I don't know. I'm worried about the blowback."

"Well, people understand your position and your responsibility. As you said, they aren't tied to ancient religious ideas. They are progressive and freethinkers. I'm sure it will go well."

"I hope so."

Chapter 8
The First Meeting

In the Slarone Center, two television cameras connected every home, business, restaurant and bar with the meeting. There was a large, half-moon table of dark, shiny mahogany. It was big enough to span the thirteen cushioned chairs that sat in a semicircle around its border. The straight side faced the cameras and attendees. That way, everyone could be seen at once, and no position was more important than another.

The first meeting began promptly at 6:16 PM local time. That is what Brian requested, and no one knew why that odd time was selected. When asked, Brian just said he liked the number 616.

From the view of the audience, the thirteen entered from the curtain on the left and took their places at the table. Dr. Challhert, The Contrarian, walked in after they were seated and took his place at a desk to the right of the large round table. His location seemed like the orbit of a satellite around a larger half-moon. Upon his desk was a sign that said "The Contrarian: Dr. Gunter Challhert."

Finally, Brian Slarone emerged from the left curtain and spontaneous applause erupted. He approached the podium that was positioned in the middle of the stage. He tapped some paper on the wood and cleared his throat. He seemed somehow pensive. The audience quieted.

"Ladies and gentlemen, the members of the Decision Committee, and all you viewers at home, thank you for participating in our first meeting. I would like to get right to the point so we can all work together to solve our problems and continue to make Atheistika a beacon of light and truth to the entire world. Our first meeting here is the beginning of a remarkable adventure. On your left, you see representatives from the House of Egalitarian Law, the Civil Rights Coalition, and the Representatives of Atheistika's districts. But, I am sure you have noticed one other person. He slowly swept his hand toward Dr. Challhert who responded with a nod.

"As you all can see, we have what has become known as The Contrarian. As The Contrarian, Dr. Challhert's job is to provide input and commentary on the issues presented. His goal is to expose possible problems that we all might not immediately see. Though it will extend the decision-making process, the objective is to find long-term, logical and ethical solutions, not quick, easy fixes. He has sworn an oath to uphold his duty to the best of his ability."

He looked at Dr. Challhert and smiled courteously.

He nodded in response with an equally courteous, but subdued smile.

Brian returned his gaze to the cameras and continued. "So, I ask that you give him the respect due to the difficult task that he has agreed to carry out."

He smiled, extended his left arm towards, Dr. Challhert, and with a slight chuckle said, "And, of course, don't hold anything he says or does against him. He's just doing his job."

The chuckle was met with a continued silence from the audience.

Gunter winced internally and was reminded of the previous night's conversation with his wife.

"Dr. Challhert is well-qualified, has a Ph.D. in philosophy, and has taught courses on logic, ethics, and philosophy for over 20 years in Florida. He's a part-time teacher here at Slarone College."

Brian paused for a moment and looked at Dr. Challhert who again smiled back with an appreciative nod.

"I want to make it perfectly clear that all the issues that have been raised by the Civil Rights Coalition will all be addressed. We will examine them and offer solutions. Undoubtedly, we will run into disagreements, but with reason, cooperation, and a healthy cross-examination, we will promote the social well-being of all the citizens of Atheistika along with an equitable distribution of the assets of our Island Nation for the common good."

Brian retrieved a paper that had been resting on the podium and then nodded to someone off stage to his left.

A large projection screen slowly lowered from the ceiling behind him. When it was down, the list of issues proposed by the CRC appeared.

Brian looked around the room one more time and then over to the half-moon table with its residents. After a bit of a dramatic pause, he said, "Well, let's get this thing started."

Chapter 9
Nothing Much To Say

The first few meetings consisted mainly of discussions about the restrictions on personal property ownership and development, procedures for a more efficient system of filing complaints, term limits for members of the House of Egalitarian Law, the break up of the monopoly of One Bank, provision for the elderly who became destitute, financial support for those who had lost their jobs, restrictions on how much power corporations could achieve, the formation of an environmental oversight committie, and increased taxes in order to pay for it all. That last topic caused some antagonism from most everyone who did not like the idea of more money being deducted from their paychecks.

Nevertheless, the meetings continued and solutions were offered, rejected, adopted, and voted on. But, more laws were passed and more money had to be spent. This meant increased taxation which was not met favorably by the population. The House of Egalitarian Law said that it was the only way to make the proposed solutions possible. So, after much arguing, and the assistance of persuasive interviews and commentary provided by the news media in favor of the redistribution of wealth, the population slowly acquiesced and the tax rate was raised to roughly 30%. But, it left a lot of people with a simmering negativity.

Occasionally, Gunter had been offering various comments. His words were considered, but they didn't have much impact on the final decisions made by the committee. It became a pattern to politely acknowledge his input, but dismiss it nonetheless. This, of course, was embarrassing to him and it did not reflect well on Brian.

That is why one day Brian summoned him to his house for a chat. It was the first time he had been there, and Gunter knew to take it seriously. He sat stiffly in a soft, cushioned chair opposite Brian. The living room was tastefully decorated with an off-white theme that was punctuated by occasional vases of flowers and paintings on the walls. Under one of them, on an obviously expensive table was an exquisite glass sculpture of dolphins jumping out of the ocean. The open windows let the air flow in as well as the light that flooded in and illumined the soft colors of the room. It reminded Gunter of something he might see in a magazine.

"Gunter, I really appreciate your being in the meetings, but quite frankly, I'm becoming concerned that your input is not helping." Brian's tone was soft and patient.

Gunter responded with measured words. "To be honest, I'm beginning to feel a little useless up there not saying much. It's just that the first few topics about law and its procedures are out of my scope of expertise. I don't want to speak where I don't have sufficient knowledge and thereby weaken my credibility when later topics arise dealing more with ethical issues. I can assure you when those topics arise I will be far more vocal and involved.

Brian nodded slowly, the index fingers of his hands formed a triangle that rested under his chin. “Can I ask how?”

“Well, with respect, I really don’t want to get into it here, but I can assure you that the proceedings will become rather lively.”

Instantly, Gunter regretted his comment. It could be considered dismissive, and he hoped Brian did not take it that way.

After about ten seconds, he responded with a slightly firmer tone. “I think I understand. But,” he said after he adjusted himself in his chair, “I’m beginning to be a little embarrassed. After all, having a Contrarian was my idea. So, you can see how this might reflect on me.” Brian concluded his words with a direct stare into Gunter’s eyes.

He swallowed and quickly responded. “The next topic deals with the right of self-protection and gun ownership. I can assure you that I will be more vocal.”

“Excellent,” responded Brian with a small tone of relief woven into the word. He continued to look Gunter in the eye. “But, I hope you won’t be too vocal.” With that, Brian stood up, faced a large window, and gazed out into the beautiful ocean scene.

“I know you’ll do well.”

Chapter 10
The Sixth Truth

The meetings had been going smoothly. The general consensus was that they were a bit boring and as a result, the attendance had been dwindling. Tonight, the sixth topic, the right of self-protection and gun ownership was on the table. That is when Gunter's philosophical commentary would become more evident. It was just as well too because with Brian's urging to become more vocal Gunter finally felt ready to uphold his office of The Contrarian with more determination.

At about 6:14 pm the room became silent and two minutes later, Shelie, who had become the unofficial spokesperson, jumped right in and got things started.

"We know Brian has stated there will be no guns allowed on the island. But, unfortunately, we have seen a slow, but steady rise in crime and people have asked about weapons being used for self-protection. Though I agree with Brian and believe we should ban guns altogether, the issue has been raised, and since we are a Democratic Socialist system where the people have a say, we will now discuss this issue."

Her tone was matter-of-fact.

She looked down at a piece of paper.

"There have been several instances of home invasions. In one of those, an older gentleman was alone when a masked intruder assaulted him, tied him up, and robbed him. He needed to be hospitalized, but he will be fine. Then there's a report of a single woman who was awakened by noises one night. After shouting, "Who's there?" She said she heard what sounded like two people fleeing her home. She, of course, is now having trouble sleeping and wants a dog."

Shelie paused for a moment before clearing her throat and examining the audience.

"As it stands only our police force has guns, and all of the weapons are accounted for. But, unfortunately, there have been reports of illegal guns on the island. This is very disconcerting. Their existence has not been verified and is nothing but rumor so far. The police are looking into it."

The last statement caused a subtle wave of whispering to spill through the crowd.

Shelie fingered some papers and shuffled them loudly enough to be heard in the auditorium, signaling their silence.

"I have obtained a police report about crime statistics on the island. In the past three months, there have been five reports of break-ins at small businesses. There have also been 11 instances of the theft of bicycles, purses, wallets, etc. There have also been three car break-ins. Given the rise of crime, many citizens want to protect their property as well as themselves. This is why there is a request among many of the residents to have weapons – with the requisite registration and training, of course."

Shelie walked over to the main table with a

stack of papers with the proposition to consider gun ownership. She handed it to the closest person and returned to the podium.

"Just to be clear, I am not in favor of allowing any guns into the hands of anyone besides our policie force. I believe I speak for most people in Atheistika on this matter. Personally, I think they would only contribute to the problem. However, though the number of people requesting weapons is small, their requests need to be addressed."

She then turned and faced Gunter and matter-of-factly asked, "Does The Contrarian have anything to add before we proceed?" Her expression was blank and her tone almost condescending.

The sudden change of focus caught him off-guard. He adjusted his posture and cleared his throat. Now was his chance to be heard. After fumbling through a few pieces of paper, he found one, gathered his thoughts, stood up slowly, then walked up to the podium.

"I read to you from the Ten Truths, number six. 'Morality is to be determined by both reason and the consensus of the population where we seek the betterment of humankind and reduction of overall harm.'"

He put the paper down and absentmindedly positioned its bottom edge parallel to the edge of the podium. Then he looked up.

"The issue here is reducing overall harm. Now, we all believe in reason as a necessary means by which we can improve our lives and increase well-being. But, there is a problem we must watch out for."

Gunter picked up and fingered the same piece of paper in front of him again as he glanced out at the audience. He knew that what he was about to say could be incendiary.

With a deep breath, he began.

"Before I tell you what the problem is, let me remind you that my job here is to be The Contrarian. Therefore, in keeping with the oath of my office, I must speak."

He glanced over at Brian who was intently watching him, then back to Shelie, the 13, and then finally he focused on the audience.

"The Sixth Truth says, and I quote again, 'Morality is to be determined by both reason and the consensus of the population where we seek the betterment of humankind and reduction of overall harm.' First of all, reason deals with logic and bridging the gap between logic and morality is inherently difficult. It is what I like to call the is-ought-barrier. Just because something is logical, it doesn't mean it is also moral. Second, the consensus of the governed does not always mean that the majority opinion is the morally right one. This has the potential of leading to mob rule with the trampling of our rights. Third, without first defining what harm actually is, we can't pass laws to minimize it. After all, there are different kinds of harm such as emotional, physical, and financial. Laws that we pass would have to reflect these varying aspects of harm and be subdivided so as to cover various types. Fourth, since we have agreed to the Sixth Truth and since we want to reduce overall harm, it would seem logically fitting that if everyone possessed a weapon, then everyone would be equal and such things as robbery and physical harm, at least within one's home, would be greatly reduced, thereby fulfilling the Sixth Truth.

He cleared his throat, a bit nervous about what he was saying, aware of the calmness of his own tone.

"Nevertheless, since Brian has set up a Democratic Socialist system and since we are trying to be democratic, I recommend that we let the people vote on whether or not guns should be allowed on the island. Thank you."

Gunter then abruptly turned around and walked back to his seat and sat down with a slightly clumsy movement.

It took a few seconds for his words to sink in. Most people quickly shifted their focus from Gunter to Brian. He had just cross-examined Brian's basic edict on morality, something upon which Atheistika had, in part, been founded.

The room waited for Brian to respond.

Finally, he stood up and approached the podium, almost casually. Once there, he clenched his jaw a little and tapped the fingertips of his left hand on the podium making a slight, drumming sound.

"Mr. Challhert has carried out his duties properly, just as I have asked him to do. Therefore, I will not object to his statements. The Sixth Law still stands, and we can adhere to the majority vote."

With that, he returned to his seat and sat down with what seemed to be a strained, mechanical movement.

He had used Gunter's last name.

Shelie stared at Brian and then over to Gunter.

"Mr. Challhert, I appreciate…we all appreciate the difficult job you have. But, attacking one of the Ten Truths isn't the issue here. We want to discuss whether or not we should have guns as a form of self-protection."

Gunter furrowed his brow as he listened to her challenge. He wasted no time. He stood up once more and spoke loudly enough to be heard from where he was.

"I respectfully would like to add that I did not attack the Sixth Truth. I quoted it and merely commented based on its wording in accordance with my office. Furthermore, I am obligated to offer contradictory commentary, whether I believe it or not."

He paused briefly to give himself a second to solidify his thoughts.

"We all agree we don't want to be harmed. But just because a majority of people want something, or…" he said with a careful tone, "what one person wants, that doesn't make it morally right."

Brian's eyes locked on Gunter. The obvious slight against him triggered a low rumble from the audience. But, Gunter continued.

"If the entire world decided that the nation of Atheistika was somehow a global threat and declared war on us, then the notion of doing what is right because that's what the majority of people want, would mean that we would have to approve of their action. This is the danger of having morality established by majority vote. For us to decide the moral appropriateness of owning firearms based on the desire of the majority accomplishes nothing more than morality by majority opinion. On the other hand, if we agree that the overall reduction of harm is the primary goal, then logically we must consider the use of weapons as a means to that end. Thank you."

He sat down and then looked to his wife. He examined her subtle expression which was a combination of surprise and concern.

He pressed and rubbed his palms on his thighs as he looked through the disapproving crowd. Had he gone too far? Was he making an enemy of Brian and maybe others as well? He wasn't sure. Why did he say what he did and included Brian? Was it adrenaline? Was it anger? He shook his head slightly. But, he knew he had to speak the truth, and he hoped that everyone would understand. After all, that was his job.

Shelie once again stood up to speak.

"If I heard you correctly Gunter, you want to put the issue of gun control up to the popular vote, and you recommend that it be passed? Did I get that right?"

He rose to speak. "I'm not recommending anything except that we let the people decide."

She countered with, "But, guns are dangerous and what if the majority of people want guns. Should we allow that?"

"According to the Democratic Socialist system that Brian has set up, yes, if that is what they vote."

"And what is your personal opinion about gun control? Do you approve of guns?"

He glanced over at his wife who returned his gaze with a frozen, neutral expression.

Gunter stood up once again. He felt as though he was on trial but he knew he needed to respond wisely.

"My opinion is irrelevant here, but, since you ask, I do not approve of them. Nevertheless, in keeping with my oath to function in office as The Contrarian, I must say that there is no objective moral standard by which the Sixth Truth can be demonstrated to be universally true so as to impose it upon people. The Sixth Truth is an opinion. If everyone here wants to operate under that opinion, that is their choice. Therefore, let the people decide."

With that, Gunter sat down. He tried to swallow, but his dry throat made it difficult.

Shelie looked back at the committee and then to Brian. She was waiting for him to put a stop to this quasi-attack on the foundational principle. Others focused on him, too.

Brian stood up again, but slowly. He looked around the room and then at Gunter. With what seemed like a labored gait, he approached the podium.

The room grew silent.

"Mr. Challhert is only doing what he is supposed to do. He was polite and succinct in his delivery. I do not fault him for what he said."

With that, he looked at the audience, then

back to Gunter and said, "Well, done." It was slight, but somehow his tone didn't seem to match his words. Then he walked back to his seat and sat down as slowly and stiffly as he had stood.

Shelie perceived the slight dissatisfaction of Brian's body language and delivery. Our host has spoken." She looked at Gunter with an examining eye and then with a slower delivery said, "And so has Mr. Challhert."

Gunter knew he had upset a lot of people. Did he need to do some damage control?

"May I say one last thing?" he asked, trying to convey an attitude of humility in his tone.

"Of course," responded Shelie.

Gunter rose from his chair, inadvertently imitating the speed and style with which Brian had stood up only moments ago. He approached the podium.

"My job is to look for potential problems in the issues proposed. Personally, I agree that we should enact laws that would prevent harm. But, the more laws we enact, the less freedom we will have. Therefore, we must be thoughtful in our decisions. If we cannot govern ourselves from within, then we must be governed by laws from without. Furthermore, it is true of any society that the more laws we pass, the less freedom we will have. This is something that we must be concerned about and not be too hasty to solve problems with more regulations."

He paused for a moment and exhaled as he looked down, then back to the gathering. His tone was softer. He spoke more slowly.

"Since we desire to reduce harm, and since sometimes the overall reduction of harm means to injure people in order to help them or even protect ourselves, and since we are supposed to pass laws by a majority vote of the populace, I say put it to a vote and let the people decide. This would be consistent with our democratic, socialist system."

Gunter abruptly turned around and returned to his seat. He grasped the papers on his desk, next to his chair, and aimlessly shuffled them, keeping his eyes low.

After a short while, everyone was watching Brian again to see what he would do. Obviously, he had to say something. He stood up and stayed where he was as he waited for the room to grow silent. Then with an obviously measured delivery, he said, "The reason we are here is because of the great financial advantages we have received from Inverisoft. Inverisoft is successful because of the security software that it has developed. The reason that software is successful is due, in part, to the CAT system which exposes flaws in the software and prevents problems from arising later on. As you know, this is a process I firmly support. In the early days of Inverisoft, this counter check system was often problematic, and there were many times when I considered abandoning it. But, I knew better. Likewise, in our situation here, the same checks and balance system needs to be in place. Mr. Challhert is only doing the job he has sworn to do. It may be unpleasant at times, but I believe it is necessary. And, since we are a socialistic democracy, we can put it to a vote and let the popular opinion become law."

Brian sat down slowly. He clenched his jaw as he reached for a pen. Then, rhythmically he pressed it down on his knee vertically, turning it over and over again.

Shelie looked at the camera and matter-of-factly said, "Ladies and gentlemen, I propose that we put this to a vote and see if the majority of people in Atheistika want gun ownership. If the vote reveals that they do, then we will offer a proposal for the House of Egalitarian Law by which they can draft a legal decision with appropriate restrictions and requirements, which we can then review here, before sending it back to them and they make it official."

She spoke matter-of-factly and did not look at Brian or Gunter. Then, she walked toward the front left of the stage and nodded at a tall, lanky man dressed in a suit who was sitting in the first row. On his knees was a laptop. She pointed at him.

"Mr. Smith has access to the Atheistika website. Mr. Smith, would you be able to quickly upload a form for voting so that we can ascertain the populations decision?"

He nodded confidently. "It will be ready in five minutes and I will link it to Atheistika's homepage."

"Good. The proposition should be worded as a question. 'Should Atheistika allow private citizens to own guns?' We need only yes and no options for now. This will help us move forward either way."

With that, Mr. Smith nodded again and began his work.

Shelie continued. "If I may be so bold since we know that most everyone is watching, I propose that we have a 45-minute recess and come back afterward whereupon Mr. Smith will provide us with the results of the survey." She looked at Brian who nodded approvingly.

Shelie then walked off the stage and down to the crowd where she entered a quick huddle of consultants.

Brian disappeared offstage.

Gunter avoided the gang of people that seemed to form near the bottom of the stage. Many were wagging their heads before him. He decided to use the restroom. Forty-five minutes would pass slowly.

He exited the stage and wove his way around sporadic small groups of people milling about, murmuring, discussing the evening's events. When he passed, they became silent and watched him. Some offered half-sincere smiles. Most did not.

Right before he got to the bathroom, two men approached him. One of them with a large beard said, "Well done. You did great. We're behind you."

It was a welcome oasis of praise.

"Thanks."

They watched him closely as he disappeared into the bathroom and took care of his business. As he exited, he saw the same two men accompanied by three more huddled in a solitary group. They all smiled as they nodded to him.

He returned a polite smile, and then zigzagged his way back through the crowd as he headed to the stage. He didn't say anything to anyone. That's when he realized he'd overlooked his wife. He was shocked that she had not popped into his mind, but he knew it was because he was so preoccupied with the situation. He looked for her. But, she wasn't there.

Alone.

Things took a little longer than expected, about an hour and ten minutes. But, the results finally came in and people, as if on cue, began to return to their seats. When they were all in place, Shelie again stood and waited for their silence. She then nodded toward Mr. Smith who walked onto the stage and handed her a piece of paper. He then returned to his seat.

Gunter tried to relax, but couldn't. So, he looked for Martha and found her sitting in the front where she was before. They looked at each other, and she smiled. Gunter immediately felt better.

Finally, Shelie spoke.

"Out of the 16,042 submissions on the website in response to the question, 1,925 are in favor of possessing weapons. 14,117 are opposed. That is a 78% disapproval rate. The proposal is not passed.

Chapter 11
Home

Gunter and his wife Martha didn't say much to each other at the center. After the vote was read and the meeting was over, they quickly headed out to their car. A few people nodded, others offered half-smiles, and many more obviously avoided them. Someone yelled, "Well done." But Gunter couldn't tell what was meant by it.

It wasn't until they got home that they were able to relax and after changing into something more comfortable, he and Martha sat down on the couch together and shared a bottle of red wine.

It was only then that he felt comfortable enough to finally deal with what he had said.

"That did not go well. I thought it would be pretty easy and that it wouldn't be as difficult as it was." He took a sip and put his hand on her knee.

He looked out the window into the darkness. The ocean was out there. Luckily there was a faint twilight of moonlight reflecting on the distant surface which offered a soothing sense of peace.

"Well, what do you think?" he asked. "How do *you* think it went?"

Martha twisted the glass of wine in her fingers. "Well, I think you did a great job. You did exactly what you were supposed to do. I thought that…"

"Yeah, that's the problem," he said

interrupting her. Then after a few seconds, "Sorry."

"It's okay. I know this is tough for you." Her tone was gentle.

He kept bulldozing through his thoughts, reviewing what he had said, the tone, the cadence. He shook his head.

"And did you see the people? So many of them were upset. But I was just doing my job. I was doing exactly what I took an oath to do. Why did so many try to stare me down and others avoid me? It's not right."

He sighed, then took another, larger drink of wine.

"I'm sure Brian is pissed."

Martha kept quiet. She knew he needed to talk it through. Vocalizing was his way. She knew he had to hear himself say things, to hear how the words sounded. But after commenting about the ubiquitous glares, he just stopped, turned to her, and unexpectedly said, "I was glad you were there. I needed you."

She noticed the abrupt change of topic and smiled. "Of course."

He swirled the wine, almost spilling it.

He sighed as he looked at his glass, lost in its movement.

Chapter 12
Brian and Gunter

Brian Slarone's home was modest but very nice. It had five bedrooms and a three-car garage. The grounds were well-kept, and it had a designer feel.

Gunter was sitting on a white, plush couch opposite Brian who was in a single white, upright recliner. He was slowly twisting a glass of water with lemon slices in his fingers as he tapped his foot rhythmically.

Gunter sat upright, as if at attention, with his hands to his sides. He felt like a little boy who had been summoned to the principal's office.

"That was quite a performance you gave last night," said Brian as he crossed his legs.

Gunter didn't say anything.

"The reason I asked you here was not to reprimand you or scold you. I wanted you to understand that I think it took guts for you to say what you did. And, of course, I've already received a lot of feedback. A *lot* of feedback. People aren't sure what to think. After all, I approved of The Contrarian position, and I must say, you certainly did your job."

Brian said the last few words with a single chuckle; then he sipped his water.

Gunter nervously jumped in. "Please understand that I am 100% behind your efforts here in Atheistika. It's just that you want me to do my job and I took an oath to do it. So, that's why I said what I did. I'm not attacking you or this great work you've done. But, if you want me to step down, I will. If you don't, well, just let me know what areas you don't want me to step into."

Brian took a sip and stared out the window at a passing bird. He set the glass down on a table next to the chair and with both hands adjusted his khaki pant legs, pulling them down toward his knees. He looked at Gunter and thought for a few seconds about what to say. He stood up and walked over to the window and examined the slanted rays of the sunlight that broke through the clouds and painted gold and silver across the ocean surface. His back was to Gunter. Then, after a full, long minute, Brian spoke.

"No, I don't want you to do anything differently. I'm very serious about what we have going on here, and I want to make sure it's done right. You did exactly what you were supposed to do, and you did it well. Whether I like it or not, you carried out the duties of your office. Good job."

Brian was still facing out the window.

Gunter responded with a subdued, "Thanks."

Brian savored the scenery.

"I love to watch the light shimmer on the ocean surface."

Gunter didn't know what to say, so he kept quiet.

Then, after a bit, Brian turned around and faced Gunter again. A kind of calm seriousness was written on his face.

"The limo will take you back to your place."

Gunter stood up, not feeling comfortable sitting. It was time to leave.

Brian stepped toward him and put his right arm out to shake his hand.

"I have things to do. I'll see you at tomorrow night's meeting. It should be interesting."

With a half-smile and a weak nod, Brian dismissed himself and disappeared into an adjacent room. Suddenly Gunter was alone.

He turned around and headed out the front door where the limo was waiting outside.

Chapter 13
Marriage

The Slarone Center was packed. Extra chairs were brought in to accommodate the overflow, but there were still a lot of people standing against the back walls and in doorways. The prospect of Gunter attacking more of the Ten Truths made things far more interesting. Everyone knew the next topic would deal with marriage and sexual orientation and almost everyone on the island was in favor of open marriage, same-sex marriage, lesbian marriage, polyamory and whatever else a person's desires demanded - as long as it was by mutual consent and didn't hurt anyone. So, when Gunter arrived with Martha, there was a semi-hush as all eyes followed them down the center aisle.

They arrived at the front row where he helped her find her seat that had been reserved for her. To assist her, he had to turn towards the audience and he could see that most everyone was watching him. He quickly perused the crowd and was met with one or two polite nods, but mostly they were stern faces staring back.

Gunter made sure his wife was comfortable and then headed to the stage to take his seat. Brian entered via the left and so did Shelie. The Thirteen were already in place.

To get things started, Brian moved towards the center of the stage to the podium and waited for silence. Shelie was patiently waiting. He looked to the crowd.

"Tonight's discussion will be on the subject of marriage and sexual orientation. And according to the responsibilities of the office of The Contrarian, Mr.Challhert will again exercise his duties and seek to find problems, or should I say potential problems, in our proposals. Shelie will again make her case in this particular area, and Gunter will, if necessary, provide his input."

Brian took a step to the side of the podium and then forward a bit, away from the mic. It meant everyone had to be extra quiet to hear him. "I want everyone to understand that Gunter is only doing his job. So, treat him with respect and please understand that he is doing something that is difficult. We spoke yesterday and I encouraged him to continue. He looked at Gunter, "I'm glad he's here."

Brian motioned slightly with his left hand towards Shelie and then moved back to his chair to sit down. She walked to the center podium and started right away.

"The topic of tonight's agenda is the issue of marriage. More specifically the proposal is that marriage is to be in accordance with one's sexual orientation including considerations on establishing the minimum age of consent.

"Though many of us assume that freedom of expression and the right to privacy, as well as the right to do with one's own body, as one sees fit, would naturally include the open-ended view of marriage. This includes marriage with people of the same gender as well as multiple partners."

She paused momentarily as she surveyed the crowd.

"It turns out that there are a lot of people, a lot of citizens, who are uncomfortable with polyamorous relationships and though they do not want to impose their opinions on others, they thought it would be appropriate to define exactly what the boundaries of marriage ought to be. They are also concerned with what has been derisively called pedophilia. They want that addressed as well as the legal age of consent for sexual activity."

She abruptly stopped and walked back to where she had been sitting. There was a small end table next to her seat. She picked up a piece of paper and returned to the podium. "Let me read from a prepared statement.

> We request that the House of Egalitarian Law consider two main issues and write proposals for lawful conditions and statements:
>
> The first issue is a definition of marriage dealing with the validity and legality of marriage contracts, including issues dealing with partners of the same sex, multiple partners, marriage with animals, and/or objects along with spousal benefits for said marriage definitions.
>
> The second issue deals with the minimum legal age of consent for sexual activity.

> Proposals for this age have been offered from as low as ten years old to as high as eighteen.
>
> Finally, though not mentioned in the CRC list of grievances and concerns presented at our first meeting, we include a request for a legal definition of civil unions where those who do not believe in traditional marriage, can enjoy the rights and privileges of said unions.
>
> We propose that definitions and laws be offered and that a vote by the populace be taken so that the citizens of Atheistika can determine, by the majority opinion, what that age of consent ought to be."

With that Shelie gathered her notes, nodded to Gunter, and said, "Mr. Challhert, do you have anything to add?"

He stood up which prompted her to concede the podium and retreat to her chair.

Gunter, who was not caught off guard this time by Shelie's abrupt address, knew the ball was in his court. He realized his words could have lasting repercussions in many areas and he was reticent to say too much. So, he rose slowly and grabbed a few papers that were on the desk next to his seat. He approached the podium as he stole a look at Martha.

She smiled lovingly. He then glanced at the random faces in the crowd and wondered what their general disposition was. But, it didn't matter. He was The Contrarian and popular opinion was not his focus.

At the podium, he placed the papers neatly side-by-side and then absentmindedly stacked them. He could feel the heavy glares and considered the importance of what he would say. How far should he go? How much should he say?

He cleared his throat and once again and continued to tend to the papers on the podium. He looked up.

"I have prepared a statement that I would like to read. I can provide copies to anyone who requests them."

He cleared his throat nervously and then jumped right in.

"I do not want to spend a lengthy time on the various details of the proposal mentioned by Shelie. So, please let me address the basic issues as they relate to our topic tonight."

"Marriage is a building block of society. Marriages reflect the morals and structure of their cultures in which they are ratified and they, in turn, affect those same societies. Therefore, how we define marriage will have long-lasting social, familial, moral, and legal ramifications in our community. There are several reasons for this. First, our children. We want them to become good, moral, and productive members of society who will be mindful of the welfare of others, work hard, and seek to minimize overall harm and increase overall happiness, not only in Atheistika but also in the whole world. Marriage definitions will have a direct impact on all of this since they will have a direct impact on familial structures, the children, and legal issues. As we define marriage, we must consider that a marriage contract helps to firmly establish the long-lasting bond of its participants more so than would a partnership without it. Furthermore, open-ended marriages, whatever that is defined to be, will have far-reaching ramifications on the children who are raised within them since, generally speaking, stable homes have a positive effect on children where unstable homes generally have negative effects. Of course, there are exceptions to this, but for the most part, stability in marriage is better than instability for the children within it."

"Second, we must consider civil unions which are actually a form of marriage but possess far less legal permanence and can support a less secure family environment. If children are brought into a civil union, then what is to prevent their parents from dissolving their union since there is far less social and legal commitment to their contract? This would be a potential hindrance to a secure home in which children need to be raised. In light of this, I recommend that marriage be defined with a more permanent legal aspect than mere civil unions would allow."

A soft rumble rose in the crowd. Gunter let his eyes aimlessly wander back and forth across the faces. He did not focus on anyone.

"Third, we must consider the ramifications of the definition as it relates to the next topic on the CRC's list "Marriage in accordance with one's sexual orientation." They are related, and so I will partially address them both here."

He paused, shifted his weight to the other leg and continued.

"We must be mindful that once we define marriage based on the vote of the population, then it will remain open to a wide variety of redefinitions in the future, thereby potentially making it meaningless. We must also consider that possible future redefinitions of marriage can inadvertently invalidate past marriage contracts and complicate the legality found within them."

"Furthermore, such pliability can lead to marriages to objects, animals, one's self, a principle, dead relatives, or whatever else a person's personal preferences may desire. Then we have the issue of polygamy, polyandry, polyamory and other variations of social and sexual unions among consenting adults. These too, must all be considered."

He turned a sheet of paper over and continued to read.

"Homosexual marriage is of particular importance and, of course, consenting adults have the right to do as they wish in the privacy of their own homes. Here in Atheistika we are excluded from the bigotry and outdated religious hierarchical structures and are free to allow loving, consenting adults of the same gender, and gender identification, to be married or not be married as they wish."

"As I have just pointed out, the potential problem of the redefinition of marriage based on majority vote means we must also address other possibilities. For example, we need to consider how might marriage could be affected by such things as a physically male person who is self-identifying as a female and marries a male. Is this then a heterosexual marriage or is it a same-sex marriage, and would it matter legally? Or, what about the age of consent - something I will address momentarily. What if a person who is physically male and is for example in his 20s or 30s, self-identifies as a 12-year-old girl and wishes to enter into a marriage contract or civil union with someone of similar physical age? Would our marriage laws permit this? Or, might this then be considered pedophilia? If yes, how might a broad definition of marriage affect pedophiles who use this as a justification for their particular sexual orientation as has the gay community and those who self-identify as any one of the multitudinous gender classifications? Then again, what if two men who each self-identify as females marry each other. Would this be a lesbian marriage or same-sex marriage or does it even matter? Though some may dismiss these considerations as needlessly detailed, they are nonetheless important since titles, ownership, powers of attorney, next of kin, legal documents, etc., can be affected by gender fluidity as they relate to the identification of persons, marriage, inheritance, and legal obligations that may change over time. One final thought on this is what happens if a physically male individual marries a physical female individual and one of them decides to physically change his or her gender or decides to self-identify as a different gender? Would this then invalidate the marriage since its original contractual agreement was between a physical male and a physical female?"

"Then there are medical concerns dealing with gender identification. Let's consider a situation where a male who identifies as a female is in a hospital and does not want to be tended to by a male nurse, but only female nurses? Would this matter at all, or should we ignore the person's preference and risk a lawsuit?

"Considerations such as these might seem unnecessarily detailed or even ridiculous. But in the wide variability of personalities on Atheistika, they may very well become issues that may affect the stability of our society in ways that we cannot presently foresee. Therefore, in order to stabilize our society now and for the future, I recommend that marriage be defined in the narrowest and strictest sense with an emphasis on the permanence of gender identity unless legally changed, including a review of the validity of a marriage should that a partner's identity change, and also include a not-so-easy means of breaking the marriage contract by divorce. Again, this brief analysis is to encourage discussion on familial stability, a more secure home for children, a reduction of unforeseen future problems for partners and families, all with the goal of producing a more stable society."

He paused for another moment before continuing. He noticed that a steady murmuring that had been ongoing during his talk. But it was still subdued.

"Regarding the legal age of sexual consent. This must be considered with the utmost care since the emotional health of the young is at stake and since it also raises the issue of pedophilia. Even now on the mainland of many countries, pedophiles are using the same arguments based on their sexual orientation as are presented by those in the LGBTQ community to justify the carrying out of their desires according to their sexual orientation which, if combined with the fluidity of gender identification, and age identification, naturally poses some potential risks."

Gunter paused as several disapproving groans rose from the audience. He ignored them.

"Regarding the age of consent. Though we appreciate the youth here on this island, we mean no disrespect to them when we, as adults, recognize that they are naïve and often misinformed. These deficits can lead to many bad decisions and long-lasting harmful ramifications. We need only think of our own early teenage years for verification of this. Therefore, I recommend that the legal age of sexual consent be 17. Thank you."

With that, he grabbed his papers and summarily returned to his seat.

It was quite a statement, and the crowd was surprisingly subdued since the collective voice handn't yet formed. People were looking at each other and then at Brian.

Someone finally broke the awkward silence and shouted, "We are not pedophiles!"

Another voice from the back, "Get rid of him."

Brian was already walking to the podium. He held his hand up and waited. Everyone complied.

"Gunter has once again given us something to think about. Thank you. I don't see any real problems or issues that we can't work through. So, let's adjourn for the evening and let the House of Egalitarian Law collect their notes as usual and offer a proposal after all of these proceedings."

He paused for a full ten seconds as he tapped his fingers on the podium and stared aimlessly at some point on a far wall.

"Let's schedule our next meeting for three days from now. Thank you all for coming and good night."

Brian turned away from the crowd and gave only a brief glance at Gunter as he walked away.

Chapter 14
Violence

Gunter took off his jacket and tie and hung them up in the closet. He kicked off his dress shoes and undid his buckle. After slipping out of his pants, he hung them up next to his jacket before he tossed his shirt in the dirty laundry basket. Then he found something casual and comfortable to wear.

In the bathroom, he stared at himself in the mirror. The neon light seemed unusually harsh and a few new lines seemed to pop out of his face along with a rogue vein in his neck. With a long exhale, he dropped his head down and placed his hands on the edges of his sink. Then, after briefly reviewing what he had said that evening, he strengthened himself, straightened up, and headed out to the living room.

Martha had taken her usual place on the couch. The coffee table had a glass of red wine on it waiting for him. She was curled up under a soft, light blanket gently swirling her glass. He plopped heavily down on the couch. She carefully balanced the glass in the air as he did.

"Well," he said, jumping right in. "How do you think it went?"

Martha stalled by taking a sip.

"I think you did a great job."

"I appreciate your kindness, but I need the truth. What do you *really* think."

She repositioned herself under the blanket and faced him more directly.

"Seriously. I think you made a lot of people angry when you compared pedophilia to homosexuality." With that she was silent.

Gunter winced slightly at her jab. His eyebrows shot up. Then, after a reflective moment, he said, "Well, I didn't exactly compare them, but I can see how it could appear like that. The fact is that difficult things need to be said, and we must seriously consider this issue of marriage. My job as The Contrarian is to do exactly that. But, I just don't like the…"

There was a sudden, loud, high-pitched, shattering crash from behind them that ripped apart the calm. Martha flinched and spilled her wine on her blanket and Gunter jumped up to face the blast of sound.

Behind them, a large rock was rolling across the carpeted flooring and stopped after it banged against a wall. The window pane had wracked loudly against the floor as shards of glass fell on the hard surface of a nearby table.

Gunter watched it all till the commotion finally quit as suddenly as it had begun. He glanced at Martha to make sure she was okay, then looked back at the rock.

He glanced out the window waiting for something else to happen. Martha was already standing up holding onto his arm. Gunter started to move toward the broken window as he let her hands pull away from his arm.

Crash! Another breaking window shattered the

silence as a second rock flew across the room and slammed into a wall before falling to the floor.

Both of them backed away.

Then, quiet once again.

They remained still, waiting.

After a few moments, Martha moved next to Gunter and pressed her body against his, clutching his arm tightly. They waited.

Silence.

They waited longer. Nothing. Still nothing.

After what he thought was sufficient time, he pulled free of Martha and moved toward the window and tried to see if anyone was outside in the darkness. There was enough moonlight to see pretty well. But there was no one out there.

Was it over? He moved back over to Martha and embraced her. She buried her face in his chest, and he then felt the release of her rhythmic sobs and the wetness of her tears upon him.

With a heavy breath and a clenched jaw, he stared out into the darkness. His anger and adrenaline pulsed through his veins.

Chapter 15
Abortion

The Slarone Center was once again filled to capacity. The overall mood was tense. Conversations sprang up like small fires in a forest of people, fueled by Gunter's statements at the previous meeting. People were of different opinions, and occasional verbal jabs were exchanged. It was evident that the energy was up as people pressed into the room to hear more controversy from The Contrarian on tonight's, emotion-filled, subject.

Once again Gunter entered with Martha. But this time, he was stiff in both his gait and expression and avoided eye contact. Instead, he gripped her hand firmly but gently, remembering the violence to his home. He knew it was because of what he said.

Just as before, he helped Martha to her chair in the front row and kissed her.

"Are you going to be okay?" he asked tenderly?

"Yes," she said. "I'll be fine."

Gunter was worried about her safety and did not want her to suffer because of him. He let out an exasperated exhale and looked into her eyes without saying a word. He held her gaze for a few long seconds.

"I love you," he said as he squeezed her hand reassuringly. "Sorry about all of this."

“It's okay.” Her response was filled with gentleness. She was a dedicated wife, full of goodness and kindness. It made Gunter all the more determined to do his job. He wanted to show her he was a man of integrity and strength.

Then he turned to head to the stage, but she pulled him back. “I know you’re still upset about what happened, but don’t let it get the best of you. Don’t let them win.”

He gritted his jaw. She could see the flex of his muscles in his face. “I won’t,” he said in a monotone.

He pulled away from her gently and headed towards the stage. Martha watched him and frowned ever so slightly as she put her fingers on her lips.

Once in position, Gunter sat and scoured the audience. To his surprise, several people had rainbow flags and rainbow T-shirts. A few held makeshift signs that read, “Homosexuality is not pedophilia,” “Abortion is a right,” “Pro-Choice,” and “Don’t deny a woman’s right to choose.”

Obviously, his words from three nights ago had been met with disagreement and from the signs tonight, he knew that there was going to be more anger aimed at him. People did not like what he had been saying.

The rocks through his windows had proven that. Would more be coming?

He crossed his legs and looked at Martha. She was talking to a man in a suit who was towering over her.

A movement in the audience caught his attention, and so he looked again at the makeshift signs. Another one, above the heads of those in the rear, appeared and seemed to walk on its own as it began to move towards the front. It said, "Sexual orientation is not a choice." He looked back to Martha who was still talking to the stranger. She seemed a little pensive. Gunter furrowed his brow.

He believed in truth and the responsibility of doing what was right. He had vowed to carry out the duties as The Contrarian and so he would. Atheistika was too important. He wanted their new nation to be a beacon of truth and light to the world. But it would not be easy. He knew that. So, he reviewed why he was there one more time and also remembered the violence to his home.

He gritted his teeth and tapped his fingers on the armchair.

But, he had to let it go. He didn't want his anger to cloud his judgment. What they did was wrong. But, he could not let it affect his job. This was too important.

He scanned the crowd looking for clues as to who might be the guilty person or persons. It was a futile effort, but he didn't care. Somehow it made him feel as though he was fighting back.

Finally, Brian appeared from off stage. He walked quickly to the podium where he adopted statuesque pose and stared out at the crowd. It signaled the room to become quiet. It did after about 30 seconds.

In each of the previous meetings, he was dressed in casual, but stylish clothing. Tonight, however, he was dressed in a perfectly-tailored, dark grey suit. The obvious formality spoke to the crowd almost as much as his words.

"I thank everyone again for showing up. Here we are once more seeking to work through the problems of our developing nation. As usual, we will have our meeting, and proposals for adjustments will be offered to the House of Egalitarian Law."

"But, there is a problem," he said as he gently slapped the podium, sending a soft audible thud into the room.

"Unfortunately, there are those here in Atheistika who don't appreciate the difficulty of Gunter's position. There are those who want to silence him and have used violence instead of voice to counter his words."

He paused and perused the audience that was now emitting a kind of soft, confused whisper.

"Three nights ago, Gunter and Martha's home was vandalized. Two rocks were thrown through his front windows. Thankfully they were not injured. The police are investigating."

The whispers changed to mildly shocked tones and indistinguishable comments. A single, unidentifiable male voice rose from somewhere in the crowd, "He deserved it." But, his comment was definitely not the sentiment of the majority. Someone else responded, "Shut up!"

Brian looked down and shook his head as he placed both hands on the sides of the podium and leaned forward.

"Alright. Alright. Please."

He took a short, deep breath and released it.

"I consider this attack upon him and his wife

to be an attack upon me personally. I am the one who insisted on the office of Contrarian, and I am the one who encouraged him to speak up."

Brian scoured the audience. His delivery became rhythmic. "This kind of behavior is not acceptable." He thumped his hand on the podium as he emphasized each word.

"If we find out who did this, they will be prosecuted to the full extent of the law and will be required to make restitution equal to twice times the cost of the damages."

Brian paused and leaned back a bit, relaxing his posture slightly. He let the silence hang awkwardly in the air.

"Gunter has done his job well, and I applaud him for it."

Another brief pause as he exhaled once again in a controlled fashion.

"It is a very difficult position he is in. Here in Atheistika, we need to have freedom of expression and the right to disagree with each other without fear of reprisal or false accusation. No one should try to silence someone else for voicing contradictory opinions, especially when it is in the completion of his sworn duties as The Contrarian."

"I heard it said once that those who demand tolerance the most are often the least tolerant. Is this the case here? Did we not come to Atheistika to escape the intolerance of religious oppression and avoid the hatred and fanaticism of those who are irrational and narrow-minded? Yes, we did. So, let's all live up to the standards of our convictions and allow freedom of expression without fear of reprisal. If you disagree, that is fine. But do so peaceably and if that doesn't sit well with you, then perhaps you should consider leaving Atheistika."

That last comment caused another mild surge of commotion to ebb through the people. Brian ignored it and turned to face Gunter, speaking over the collective voices. With a slight nod of his head, he said, "I thank you for your excellent service." Then, without saying anything more, he stared once again at the audience for several seconds before he returned to his seat on the stage.

Gunter had nodded back. His public recognition helped him feel better.

Shelie, as if activated by some invisible queue, approached the podium. Her heels clicked on the wooden floor as she approached. She wore a black blouse with a tight grey skirt and black high heels. Her brown hair was woven into a nicely pulled ponytail. She looked at Brian.

"Thank you for your words of wisdom. We all here appreciate what you have to say."

She turned to Gunter. "Please understand that the great majority sympathize with your situation and we apologize that you experienced vandalism to your home. The attack upon you in the destruction of your property is reprehensible. It should never have happened, and I sincerely hope that you and your wife never have to suffer through such intolerance and bigotry again. Let's leave that to the religious right. Furthermore, I hope that those who have committed this crime will be brought to justice."

She shifted from one hip to another as she

turned back to the crowd. Then after letting the silence hang in the air just as Brian had, she finally got down to business. She was, after all, a woman of direct address. Her movements were efficient, direct, and almost robotic as were, to some degree, her words. It was obvious why she had become the de facto spokeswoman given her single-minded and intelligent manner.

"Tonight's agenda is a simple topic: abortion on demand. So, I will make this quick. We at the CRC propose that abortion be a right of all residents, all female residents of Atheistika and that decisions to terminate unwanted pregnancies rest completely with the woman throughout the entire duration of her pregnancy. Therefore, we propose that the House of Egalitarian Law write a proposal stating that an abortion may be obtained at the sole discretion of the woman without cost to her at any time she chooses. After all, a woman has a right to do with her body as she desires and she should not be forced to undergo an unwanted pregnancy."

Shelie finalized her statement with a slight increase in volume.

She continued.

"This is an emotionally charged topic and I am sure it will be met with contradictory opinions, accusations, and even anger. But, remember, everyone is to behave respectfully."

She turned to face Gunter. "The floor is yours." Then, she returned to her seat.

All eyes then focused on him. He slowly rose from his chair and walked directly, purposefully to the podium, carrying a few papers with him. Once there, he placed them neatly in the center, adjusted his glasses, and put both his hands on the edges as he leaned slightly forward to scan the audience. Before he spoke, once again the image of the shattered window and fearful sobs of his wife filled his mind. He grit his teeth and tapped on the podium, then forced himself to dismiss them. He had a job to do.

"I have sworn an oath to carry out my duties to the best of my ability and I will do that. Therefore, as The Contrarian, I will say things that I will not personally believe, yet are consistent with the oath that I've taken."

He paused and pressed his fingertips into the wood of the podium as he considered his next words.

"I spent time writing a statement, but I have decided not to read it. Instead, I will speak from my heart. I hope you will bear with me as I address this issue of abortion."

He turned the stack of papers over and put his hands on the podium's edges again and unconsciously tapped the fingers of his right hand.

"This topic is very volatile. We have all seen how many religious bigots, and I might add, even some secularists ones, have sought to deny the rights of women to do with their bodies as they see fit."

His tone was strong.

The audience was silent.

"Now, whether we like it or not the world is watching and how we represent women's rights and the very nature of life itself will have long-lasting ramifications. So, though we may, in a knee-jerk fashion, simply state that a woman must have the right to abortion upon demand, and since my job is to offer something to the contrary, I must now speak. And, in so doing I will speak not only to you, but also to the world."

Silence, still.

He slipped into teacher mode without realizing it. A few more seconds of his quiet allowed him to calm himself just a bit more. Then, with a noticeably softer tone…"

"Death comes to us all. For some, it is expected. For others, it is not. But for all of us who have lived our years through trials and tribulations, we understand that our lives and the lives of others are important to us. When the sleep of death awakens, it shall claim us, every one of us. Therefore, we ought to cherish life while we have it. But, not only this, we are also the highest species that evolution has produced on this planet. We are special, and our unparalleled existence has been purchased by the death of countless millions of our ancestors. Therefore, we ought to value the life we have because getting here has taken a very long time, and once we die, the only thing left is our footprints in history."

"Now, most everyone agrees that life is precious. That's why we seek to preserve our own as well as the lives of others. In fact, we call it being humane when we talk about the proper treatment of animals. We seek to treat them well because they are a lower form of life in the evolutionary chain and since we value our lives, we also ought to value theirs. After all, we are separated only by an evolutionary tree and more complex brains."

He swallowed hard and once again flushed away the memory of the rocks crashing through his living room windows that had seemed to constantly surface as he spoke. He furrowed his brow slightly as he looked at Martha, then back to the audience.

"So now let me speak difficult words, words that are in keeping with my office of The Contrarian, words that we must consider in light of the value of life itself, all life."

"We seek now to address the issue of abortion which is, no matter what anybody says, the termination of life. Because it is life and since we also claim to value life, our laws ought to reflect a consistent value of life whether it be animal or human, old or new."

All eyes were on him.

"Please consider that the life in the womb has value because it is alive. And, it has potential human life. It has human DNA. It is not a dog. It is not a cat. Even at conception, all that is there for human development is present."

He exhaled sharply and almost recoiled at the thought of where his words would lead. But it was his job.

One more controlled breath.

"As The Contrarian, I must again say that human life is inherently valuable, and we have laws designed to protect it as well as punish those who immorally and illegally destroy it or damage it. The imposition of punishment either by the antiquated death penalty or confinement and monetary fines is the result of their crimes, not their innocence."

"In light of this, how then are we to consider the life in the womb? Killing it must be done for a reason. In our discussion, the reason would be the desire of the woman. It is that desire that deems the life worth keeping or not. But, we must ask. Is it human or not? Do we impose upon it a lesser inherent value than say a rat, a goldfish, or cauliflower so that its disposal becomes easy? What will the answer to those questions say about us and how the world sees us?"

He paused for a moment and quickly surveyed the crowd. To his surprise, it was calm.

"But if it is not human, even though it is in a human womb, then what is it? When does it become human and how do we know when this change occurs?"

He took another, quick breath.

"Here is a problem. We ought to know when this life changes from non-human to human since we do not want to unintentionally kill human life. Furthermore, we must ask if the life in the womb, and it is most definitely life, has inherent value or is its value dependent upon the desires of the mother? All of these issues are clues to the fabric of our worldview, will undergird our future decisions, and will reveal to the world what we think of life itself. And, since so many in the world are religious and oppose abortion, the answers to these questions will have long-lasting ramifications on our business relations and our economy. Therefore, we must be careful and thoughtful in our decisions."

The crowd which had been for the most part

quiet and motionless was no longer tranquil. Gunter could hear the indistinguishable tones of disapproval. He took a strong, calming breath and continued.

"We must, as a nation, as an atheist nation, consider very carefully how we legislate the treatment of all life, including the most defenseless of life, life in the womb."

A woman stood up in the back and yelled something undiscernable. A few others were talking, but again, he couldn't make them out. Surprisingly, they were shushed by some people. Gunter raised his hand with his palm facing forward. It was the first time he had done that, and it worked surprisingly well.

"The world is watching, and whether we like it or not, a great many people are opposed to abortion, and they run businesses. What we do here regarding abortion can affect how they do business with us. Therefore, it is incumbent upon us to think of our financial future and acknowledge that it is becoming increasingly tied to outside corporate entities and individually owned businesses. We must consider the economic impact of our decisions very seriously."

He looked to Brian who sat stiffly in his seat, eyes locked on Gunter. He again examined the assembly and tried to read its mood. But, that too was not possible.

He looked to Martha. Her face was a mixture of concern and contemplation.

"Therefore, I propose that we consider restrictions on permitting abortion."

Gunter was surprised by his last statement. He almost retracted it but decided not to backtrack.

As equally surprising was the silence that met his last statement until after a few seconds, one person said, "Shut up and sit down," which was followed by another who, to Gunter's surprise, said, "Let him speak."

Gunter, having the advantage of amplification, raised his voice slightly.

"Only those who fear truth and the freedom of speech that brings it, seek to silence those who speak to the contrary."

Gunter paused once again to let the last comment sink in. Then, he continued in a surprisingly calm voice.

"One final thought. We must consider the ramifications of our view of life as it relates to the infirm and the mentally diminished. If we lessen the value of life in the womb, might we do the same to those who are already born and are a drain on our resources? After all, doesn't this affect the next topic of a future meeting dealing with doctor-assisted suicide?"

"This is stupid," shouted a woman from somewhere to his left. A male voice yelled indistinguishable syllable in an obviously harsh tone; then another person joined in. There were respondent "shushes" that were met with even more negativity.

Again, that same voice from somewhere said, "Let him speak."

Gunter pressed his fingertips to the podium so that his knuckles became white.

"I am only offering points to consider in light of my sworn duties as The Contrarion. Do with them as you will."

"Go to hell!" shouted someone. A few people started to stand up and yell, but their words were lost in the disorder of several people who were shouting over each other.

Brian, by this time, had risen and was already moving towards Gunter. Once next to him, he nudged towards the mic. Gunter gave way.

"Everyone calm down. Calm down."

He waited for the momentum of anger to lessen.

Gunter's heart was pounding. He looked at Martha who was obviously worried. She glanced around nervously.

He had just thrown a philosophical rock into their collective pool. With a purposeful exhale, he took a few more steps backward as if distancing himself from the mess he had made.

Brian held both hands up towards the crowd and waited for the people to calm down. After about 20 seconds, he put his hands on the podium.

"Gunter has said some pretty difficult things. Of course, we know that a woman has the right to do with her body as she sees fit."

Was Brian doing damage control? Wondered Gunter.

Someone shouted an insult. Another joined in. The word bigot could be heard, as well as "religious nut." Brian raised his hand again and waited for silence once more. He looked to Gunter and then back to the crowd.

Then to everyone's surprise, a man yelled, "Screw you, Brian." Another yelled, "Yeah!"

The shock of those words silenced the crowd momentarily. Brian stopped in his tracks and stared into it, then back to Gunter who had taken another step back.

Brian faced the crowd and raised his hands, but this time, it took even longer for silence to manifest, too long.

He stared, frowning, his jaw positioned forward a little, pressing his front teeth together.

"I propose that we take an adjournment and wait a full week before we continue. It is obvious that we need to review everything more carefully. We must consider our next actions and decisions thoroughly. This meeting is adjourned."

Brian stepped away from the podium and turned to Gunter and said with a monotone, "Tomorrow. My house. Noon." Then, he disappeared off stage.

Gunter watched the crowd begin to disperse, glad that no one was heading his way. Martha was lost in the shuffle, but he knew he'd find her shortly.

What had he done? Why did he say so much? He had always believed in the right of a woman to choose what to do with her own body, but he had just challenged that. He shouldn't have. Yet, at the same time, it needed to be said, and there was something in him that told him he had spoken the truth.

That puzzled him.

Chapter 16
Brian and Gunter Again

Gunter sat sheepishly in the soft, plush chair opposite Brian who was twisting a glass of water in both hands as he examined Gunter. There was a mangled slice of lemon descending to the bottom.

Suddenly, a cell phone rang in Brian's pocked breaking the awkwardness. He reached in, took it out, rejected the call, and dropped it onto the end table next to his chair. Then he looked again at Gunter.

"That was quite a performance last night. A lot of people are really upset. I've received a ton of emails demanding that you be expelled from Atheistika.

Gunter flinched slightly.

On the other hand, a quite a few people agreed with you. But, mostly its been a series of complaints. In fact, we have been getting emails from all over the world. Many on the religious right are praising you, though with reservations. And, then again, you have received a few death threats from several places."

Gunter jutted his head forward a bit and frowned. Brian's last sentence was unexpected. Death threats? Why?

Brian twisted his water glass again. "You're famous."

Gunter said, "Or infamous."

Brian set the glass down on a coaster on the table next to his chair with a soft thud. He examined his guest behind his almost imperceptible frown.

"Do you have anything you want to say?"

Gunter jumped right in. "To be honest, I'm surprised at the reaction. I didn't do anything except give counter-arguments and raise concerns – just like I was supposed to do. I didn't *mean* to be incendiary."

"I believe you," said Brian. His words carried a kind of restraint woven into the syllables. He crossed his leg. "But, obviously you upset a lot of people. I had hoped you would have fully supported our positions here instead of undermining them."

Gunter winced at the sting of rebuke. He thought about the broken windows, the fear and suffering imposed on Martha, and how he had simply challenged peoples' assumptions and looked for potential problems. He was just doing his job. That's all. But, now was not the time to push his self-justification. Now was the time for a different tact.

"I'll admit, I've had time to think about it, and well, maybe I was still in a bit of shock from my home being violated. And seeing what it did to Martha, my anger, the crowd, well, all I can say is that I think I was more upset than I realized. I just started talking, and it all came out. I…I'm sorry. I don't know what else to say. I screwed up."

Gunter adjusted himself in the seat, nervously, waiting for a verbal guillotine to fall. He decided to pre-empt it. "Of course, I can no longer be The

Contrarian. That is obvious. You'll have to find someone else if you want to keep this procedure going."

A bird flew by the window and distracted Gunter for a moment. He let out a strong exhale. "I'm really sorry."

Brian grit his teeth and exhaled slowly as he rose from his chair and walked over to the window. He stared at the ocean as he so often did, waiting for the calming waters to soften his displeasure.

"If put so much into Atheistika. So much."

Gunter waited like a child ready to be scolded again.

"There are reports that a protest has formed outside the Slarone Center. I don't know why, but we are looking into it. There have also been reports of vandalism, here and there, as well as graffiti, a lot of it aimed against you personally…and some at me. People are angry."

He shook his head.

"And, believe it or not, there are people here who agreed with what you said. Your words have polarized our nation. And, I hate to say it, but this whole thing isn't working out with you as The Contrarian."

Brian shook his head and said, "I don't get it. We've got a great thing going here on our island home. Why the hostility?"

He delivered the question with a slowness that belied contemplation.

Then, as if passing a hurdle, he turned and faced Gunter. "I've decided to continue with the meetings, but your services will no longer be needed. In fact, this whole Contrarian idea is finished. We need to move forward more quickly, and we certainly don't need any more problems. People are not computer programs. I was wrong to insist on The Contrarian idea."

Gunter slumped in his seat, struck by the words that obviously pointed to his failure.

"Again, I apologize."

Brian turned back to the window.

Gunter stared at the back of Brian's head, then down to the empty chair as he reviewed last night's meeting. It had not gone well. And, how would it affect his life on the Island? Would things blow over? Or, he thought, maybe he would no longer be welcome. He didn't know. He and Martha had moved and committed to living here, but after last night, maybe that wasn't going to work out. Were they safe? Suddenly it occurred to him that maybe they weren't. He thought of Martha and how all of this was going to affect her. The protests and violence meant there was an underlying current of…"

"Gunter? Gunter?"

Brian was calling his name. "Are you there?"

Gunter shook himself free. "I'm sorry. I got lost in thought. This whole thing is not easy." Gunter stood up. "I think it's time for me to leave and get back to the house. Martha doesn't exactly feel safe being alone." And then, as an afterthought, "…no thanks to me."

He took a few steps towards the door before stopping and turning to face Brian. "Maybe I shouldn't say this, but, last night's reaction is not a good sign. Far too many people got way too angry and, as you said, there's the vandalism and protests. This tells me that the underlying attitudes of a lot of people are pretty bad. There isn't much tolerance, and that can have a chilling effect on society as well as lead to oppression and discord. I think I only made it surface much faster than it normally would have. Perhaps if the problems had manifested more slowly, things could have been dealt with easier."

He stared at Brian some more and said, "People behave according to what they believe. We will all see what our country is made of soon enough."

With that, Gunter was once again surprised to find that he was speaking from someplace deep within. It gave him a strange confidence. "I need to leave."

"I agree," said Brian who looked straight into Gunter's eyes as he said it.

Chapter 17
At Home Again

Gunter and Martha sat quietly at the dinner table. She had prepared a light meal but had been keeping mostly quiet. Now and then, she would put her hand on Gunter's shoulder and squeeze reassuringly as she passed by. It was both comforting and annoying.

Now, they just sat there together, not saying anything.

The previous night's debacle was hanging heavily in the air. There wasn't much to say, and they both suspected that their future on the island was in jeopardy. Of course, he had told her everything about his meeting with Brian and how he was now no longer needed as The Contrarian. That was fine. In fact, it was more than fine. He was happy to be done with it.

But now he had to deal with the fallout, and he wasn't sure what to do. Could he just continue as normal? Or, would he be ostracized and ridiculed? Would he still have a job at the college? Though he knew there were people who agreed with what he said, there were also plenty who did not and they were vocal. Then, there was the attack on his home. Would more be becoming?

He shook his head, frowning at himself, examining his own conscience and rehearsing in his mind some of the things he had said. He was a philosopher who loved exploring ideas, who valued differences of opinion and saw disagreements as tools of learning for the betterment of humankind. He believed that back-and-forth dialogue was healthy, whether easy or not. To him, polite disagreement and challenge were exactly what any mature society needed. It was part of progress. But, here on the island, that essential belief, which he considered so integral to rationality and truth, did not seem to be very popular. It frustrated him. But, he was mostly upset with himself for his own lack of wisdom. He knew he had said too much.

He looked across the table at Martha who was now sitting there absentmindedly using her fork to turn over some leaves of her salad.

Finally, with a sigh, he pulled a piece of folded paper out of his shirt pocket, placed it on the table, and tapped it with his index finger. She looked at it waiting for him to explain.

"When I got up this morning, this note had been slipped under the front door. I was waiting for the right moment to read it to you. I don't think there is one. So, let me just get it over with. He opened it up.

"We are a diverse and clandestine group on The Island that operates in obscurity because we are small in number. We agree with the general sentiment of your statements that cross-examined important issues. However, we have chosen not to speak publicly in support of you at this time, since we are not the majority, and our livelihoods would be jeopardized. Nevertheless, several in our group work in important areas on the Island, which is how we have discovered that there is a growing hostility towards you. We do not believe it is safe for you here anymore. Please take precautions."

Gunter inhaled deeply, then let the breath slowly drain out of him. He put the note back in his pocket and then focused on Martha. She didn't say anything, but her furrowed brow and sudden change of breathing spoke clearly.

"I'm sorry, honey. I did not want to tell you, but I knew I had to. You need to know what's going on."

Martha put her fork down, folded her arms, and sat back in her chair. She stared at him for about 10 seconds. Then, in a soft tone, she asked, "What do you think we should do?"

Gunter could easily read her mood. So, he responded cautiously.

"Well, we either stay and tough it out, or we go back to Florida and start over."

He pulled the note out of his pocket again and perused it once more before slipping it back in. Then he said, "I say we stay. It'll blow over, and things will work out. I do not want to be intimidated. I do not want to be forced out. This is our home."

She formed a lopsided smile. "One of the things that drew me to you was your confidence and your convictions. You're a man of integrity, and that's one of the reasons I love you so much."

With that, she went back to rearranging her salad. Gunter watched her aimless movements. Obviously she was trying to supportive, even though she was clearly upset.

Gunter sat back and stared up at the ceiling.

This whole Contrarian thing had really messed up their lives. It was sad. He tried to consider how much of it all was due to him and how much was simply because he was carrying out his duties. He didn't like that Martha was suffering because of it.

He took a therapeutic sip of wine.

Martha was still playing with the salad. He watched her fiddling as a tuft of hair fell down on her brow. Instantly Gunter's heart skipped a beat.

"I love you."

She looked at him. "Love you, too." Then, she returned to her salad.

He considered how blessed he was to be married to her. She had been loyal, long-suffering, and had endured the move to this island which was mostly his idea. She wanted to stay on the mainland close to their children. But she had followed him here because she loved him and knew how much he valued the philosophical idea of Atheistika.

All this was running through his mind. "You know something?" He said as he offered a half-smile.

She abandoned the salad for a moment and focused on him.

"You're a wonderful woman."

She smiled again, half-heartedly.

"What I said at the meeting was right. Maybe I didn't say it perfectly, but everything I've been saying for the past few meetings has been true. All I did was my job and now, now this."

He slapped his shirt pocket.

"I was right about valuing life and how it can be a slippery slope if we don't seriously consider our beliefs. Where will it stop? Sure, the woman has the right to choose, but we have to be very careful when considering where those choices will lead. We have to…"

He realized his volume had been increasing and he was starting to work himself up again, just like last night. It was as though something down deep inside of him wanted out. He pushed it away as he slid his chair back, stood up, and meandered slowly away from the table. Then, he came back to his chair and put his hands on its back.

"In all the years of teaching I've had to study truth and wisdom as well as history. Philosophy has always been embedded in different cultures, some good and some bad. Sometimes philosophers have been mistreated and even ridiculed by the populace whose narrowminded ignorance sought only safety, food, sex, and entertainment. Precious few give serious thought to the consequences of what they consider to be true or right and wrong. After all, we behave based on what we believe, not what we don't believe. That's always been true. It's vitally important that our beliefs are well-founded and based on logic and morals because it's from our beliefs that we form our actions."

He slipped into his teaching mode. But, he wasn't talking to her anymore. He was speaking to himself. He looked past her.

"It has always been throughout history that the intolerance of contrary thought reveals a society's true character or lack thereof. What I have seen in the last few days here on The Island is a demonstration of the level of health in our society.

When unpopular opinions are voiced, they are met with anger and condemnation."

He smacked the note again harder. "That is a sign that almost always precedes the fall of nations or at the very least its digression into intolerance, dogmatism, and persecution. Intolerance in the name of truth is hypocrisy and it is dangerous. Absolute intolerance leads to death. Just think of Stalin, Mao Zedong, and Hitler. They had no tolerance for dissenting ideas and the people who brought them. Millions died because of them."

Gunter picked up a glass of wine and swirled the liquid strongly, watching the legs run down the inside. Then, he downed the whole glass in one giant gulp before setting it down.

"It doesn't make sense, though. The vetting process was pretty good. So, why were the people in the meetings…"

He glanced at Martha who was quietly staring back, expressionless.

"I'm sorry, hun. I guess I'm worked up about…"

There was a sudden, loud cracking of splintering wood exploding from the kitchen. Gunter flung himself to face it. Another snap. Another loud crash. He glanced over at Martha and instinctively moved toward her. She was already stepping towards him. Then he thought of the police and lunged towards the phone. But before he could dial, he heard Martha scream. He jerked around just in time to see a masked figure moving quickly. Then, he felt a sharp crack of pain in his skull.

Everything went black.

Chapter 18
The Demand

The dim, blurry light grew in brightness as the ceiling came into focus. He squinted and noticed a sharp pain in his scalp. Gunter reached for his head and winced hard. He lifted his fingers. There was no blood. Then he bolted up. "Martha!"

"I'm okay. I'm okay," she said in a trembling voice. She was sitting on the couch next to where he was on the floor. Opposite them, two large, strong men stood like statues. They wore ski masks, dark leather jackets, combat boots, and black gloves. Each was well built and each had a bat.

Gunter slowly, carefully raised himself and sat next to Martha on the couch, considering the thugs' nonaction to be silent permission. He cautiously looked around to see if anyone else was there.

"It's just us," said one of the masks, his powder blue eyes piercing through the eye slits.

He took the bat and pointed it at Gunter, "You are no longer welcome here." He rapped the blunt end of the bat on the coffee table, leaving a dent in the wood grain.

"Do you understand me?"

For a moment Gunter considered defiance. They had busted into his home, assaulted him, and terrified his wife. "Go to hell," he said.

The talking mask slammed his bat on the coffee table harder, sending a loud crack throughout the room. He lifted it and pointed it at Martha then slowly moved it closer to her face. She whimpered and cowered back into the couch grabbing Gunter's arm.

"This is your last warning. Leave. We will be watching you. You have 24 hours."

The masked man moved the bat and placed it under Martha's jaw, then lifted her head with it. She began to cry, stuttering out the tears in fearful groans.

"Leave her alone!" demanded Gunter as he tried to swat the bat away from her. The man flicked it sideways and thudded with Gunter's temple.

"You don't give the orders here little man. You take your woman, your ideas, and leave. He brought the bat back under Martha's jaw and forced her head back again, this time more forcefully.

"Okay!" Said Gunter as he rubbed his temple. "We'll leave. Just go. We'll leave as soon as we can."

The masked man pointed the bat at him and inched it closer before stopping. He stood there motionless for several seconds. Martha choked out another whimpering cry.

"I said we'll go," declared Gunter in a more submissive tone as he stared passed the bat at the man. "We will leave. We'll leave. Just don't hurt her. Please. We'll leave. Whatever you say."

The masked man relaxed and stood up straight raising the bat to his shoulder. He peered at Martha then back to Gunter.

"24 hours."

The blue-eyed man looked over at his silent

partner and jerked his head towards the back door; then he started to move. The silent one followed. On their way out, the second man swung hard at a glass lamp, sending shards everywhere. He kicked over a chair, then attacked a family picture hanging over a piano. He glanced back as he pointed the bat at them.

Gunter held Martha close to himself.

"24 hours." He said.

The man raised the bat in the air and hurled it across the room at a china cabinet. The shattering was horrific. He then hurried out through the kitchen, and the two disappeared back into the darkness.

Martha buried her face in Gunter's chest and began to sob heavily.

Chapter 19
Fleeing

Neither of them slept that night. They did not contact the police because they didn't know who they could trust and they certainly didn't want to make things worse. Besides, it would only waste their time. She spent most of the night packing two large suitcases for each of them as well as a couple of boxes, painfully considering what to take and what to leave. Now and then she would stop and cry.

He was busy looking online for flight information. He also started emailing old friends on the mainland about their return. But, Gunter was careful not to say anything that might cause any more problems because he didn't know if his emails were being monitored.

The airport wouldn't open for a few more hours until after daybreak. So, for now, they just got organized the best they could.

Martha worked silently, slowly, wiping her eyes periodically, and angrily tossing clothing into a suitcase.

Gunter would check on her, but she was not in the mood to talk.

"We can't leave until the airport opens. The next available flight is around noon, and there are several empty seats. So, I bought our tickets. The blue-eyed man says we have 24 hours so I figure we can at least take the boxes to the post office and try to have them shipped back to the mainland. I'll send them to the University. They will hold them there for me."

Martha was quietly listening while she was packing, but she didn't look at him.

Gunter left her alone. Occasionally he tried to embrace her and comfort her. He wanted to do more to help but knew he couldn't. She received his embraces with a polite stiffness.

"I'm sorry," he said. "It's all my fault."

She didn't respond.

Her silence stung.

When they were done packing, he managed to eat something, more out of necessity than hunger. Martha was too upset for food. They put the bags and the boxes in the car at daybreak and then took one last look around the house to see if anything of particular value needed to be retrieved. But there was nothing more they could do, nothing more they could say. As they headed towards the car, they looked back at their home in quiet despair.

He put his hand on her shoulder and said gently, "Ready?"

She put her hand on his and offered a dejected, "Yes." He opened the door for her and she let herself in. He walked around to the driver's side and plopped down in the seat. She stared aimlessly out the passenger window.

He started the car and slowly headed down the driveway and turned right onto the road. Neither looked back.

"The post office doesn't open for another

hour. Once we drop the stuff off, we can go straight to the airport. We will leave the car in the parking lot and who knows, maybe from the mainland, I can arrange someone here to retrieve it and sell it. We still have some friends here, or at least I hope we do. So, it's worth a try."

Martha just watched the roadside slip by.

Gunter hated her silence and cringed internally at its subtle power.

"It's all my fault," he uttered once again, glancing over at her, examining her face, hoping for a kind word from her to make himself feel better.

She just kept staring out the window, seeing nothing.

He stared back at the road ahead of them. He didn't know why it seemed easier for him to deal with this than it was for her. Maybe it was because he felt protective and he had slipped into some fight or flight mode. Perhaps he would break down once on the mainland. He didn't know. But for now, they were leaving for their own safety, and for now that gave him something to focus on.

The post office was down the road a couple of miles. But Gunter had other plans. At the next street, he made a left.

"Where are you going?" she asked.

He welcomed her voice.

"I'm going to see Brian about this. I'm going let him know what happened and why we're leaving."

She sighed. "Do you really think that's a good idea?"

"I'm not sure. But, he needs to know why we

are leaving and that I am not abandoning him or Atheistika. In spite of all this, I still believe in it. Besides, it won't take me long to fill him in."

"I'm not staying in the car by myself. So, can we make it fast? I want to get out of here. I'm done with this place."

"Sure. I want to get out of here, too."

It only took another five minutes before they arrived at Brian's. Gunter turned into the loop-around driveway. Brian did not feel the need for security, so his home was accessible to anybody. Gunter pulled up to the front, right next to a black sedan.

He put the car in park and turned it off, then got out, and came around Martha's side of the car to help her out. They went up the steps to the large, dark, wooden door. He rang the doorbell, and they waited.

About 10 seconds later they heard someone approach, shoes clapping on the wooden floor inside. Then they watched the door slowly open. There stood a statuesque man he had never seen before - with powder-blue eyes staring back at them.

Martha suddenly had a death grip on Gunter's hand. They said nothing and neither did the man at the door who just stared at them without saying a word. Gunter took a step backward as did Martha. The man watched, expressionless, cold.

He said nothing.

They backed away slowly and turned towards the car. He helped her in as he stared at the man watching them. Then, he got in drove away. The man disappeared back inside the house.

They didn't go to the post office. They were too shaken for that. Instead, they went straight to the airport and loaded everything on carts, checked themselves in, paid huge fees for the extra boxes. Within a few hours, they were gone.

Chapter 20
The Mainland

It had been five months since they had returned to the mainland. They were staying with their oldest son and his wife. Getting their lives back together hadn't been easy. But, they were making progress.

Gunter adjusted the knot in his tie. He pulled his lapels down and checked his belt. Martha, once again, interrupted his routine and went straight for the lopsided triangle.

"They're in the living room. Are you ready?"

"Yeah," he said, exhaling the words. He kept checking his suit in the mirror. She rapped him on the shoulder to get his attention and have him face her for one final check. "Hold still."

He complied.

Once satisfied, she held him by the shoulders. "You'll do fine."

"Hope so."

She looked directly into his eyes. "Are you sure you want to do this? It isn't too late to back out."

With a measured tone he said, "Yes, I'm sure. I've given it a lot of thought, and with what's happening on the island now, I thought it would be the right thing to do."

He inspected the tie again in the mirror.

On the bed was a newspaper. Its headline

read, “Atheistika Dystopia.”

He glanced over at another newspaper next to it. “Atheistika in Distress.”

For the past couple of months, there had been more and more reports of problems on the Island. At first, they seemed trivial, but they were increasing. So, it was inevitable that the news media spent more and more time covering what was happening. But there had been some “defectors” as they were called, who had left. When asked why they didn’t say much accept that things were not as good as they used to be and decided to move on. There were rumors of increasing disorder and that some of the protests on the Island had gotten violent.

The news media tried to go to Atheistika in order to do some investigative reporting, but they were surprised to find they were not welcome. It seemed that there was a news blackout from the island. All they could do is speculate that Brian did not want negative press.

So, what was going wrong?

Brian had released some videos saying that everything was under control and that they were working out some issues. But his reassurance wasn’t convincing. As more people left and spoke about the growing problems on the Island, an increasingly dark cloud seemed to hover over its reputation. No one was sure why, but several companies withdrew their financial investments from the atheist nation. Then, as if sensing something, more and more people started to leave.

So, the news media wanted answers. That’s

why they sought out Gunter.

He turned his attention back to Martha.

"I'm sorry you have to go through all of this still. But I'm glad we're together. We'll make it." He spoke in an apologetic tone, something he had done a lot in the past few months.

"It was wonderful while it lasted," she said with a smile.

He returned her smile and checked his suit in the mirror once more.

"The university has agreed to let me teach again next semester. That's good. Though we didn't get much from the sale of our property on the island, I think it is enough for a small down payment on something. So, we should be okay."

She knew all this, but he was processing it all, restating the obvious, and preparing himself for the next hour.

He gave her another kiss, a tender kiss.

"They're waiting for you."

He nodded, made another feigned adjustment to his tie, and then headed out to the living room.

There was a news crew with equipment and lights strategically placed here and there. Two plush chairs sat in the middle of the room surrounded by three lights. He wandered a bit, aimlessly trying to find his place and not get in the way.

He moved over to one of the chairs and stood next to it, unsure which to sit in. Some tech people were doing something with wires, scurrying about, making adjustments, ignoring him. A young woman with a microphone that emerged from her hair whispered something to someone on the other end.

She locked eyes on Gunter and motioned for him to take a seat as she approached him. He complied. She introduced herself as she put a microphone on his lapel and wove the cord so that it disappeared under his jacket; then she went back to directing people.

An attractive, well-dressed woman, seemed to appear out of nowhere. She approached him and shook his hand. “I’m Ester.”

“Hello,” he said with a nod.

“I’m glad you decided to do this. The world wants to know what is happening on Atheistika.” As she spoke, a well-coifed man in his 20s delicately checked her hair.

“Well, I don’t know how much I can offer.”

“I’m sure you’ll have plenty to say. The world wants to know what’s happening.”

Behind her, Gunter could see the TV which was tuned into a local news station. The headline read, “Riots in Atheistika.”

He looked back at her. She motioned for him to take his seat, which he did. She sat in the chair opposite him.

“We’re on in one minute,” said an anonymous voice from behind him.

Gunter looked around to find Martha standing with their son and his wife. They were safely tucked out of the way of all the commotion, watching him.

The lights shone harshly into his eyes. It was uncomfortable. He tried not to squint.

Two cameras focused on him and two were on her.

Ester said, “Just be natural and talk to me.

You don't need to look into the cameras, just look at me." She smiled reassuringly. "You'll do fine."

"Okay," he said as he nodded and rubbed his palms on his trousers.

The commotion lasted for a while as Ester checked her notes. Finally, someone said, "We're on in 10, 9, 8, 7, 6, 5, 4, 3…" Then silence.

She looked directly into the camera. "Hello, I'm Ester Prowren with New World Focus. With me is Dr. Gunter Challhert, who many of you may recognize as The Contrarian from Atheistika. This evening we will be talking with him about what is happening on The Island. As you many of our viewers know, there is an increasing number of reports of riots, power outages, and sporadic violence."

Gunter's eyebrows shot up a little. He hadn't heard that.

She looked at Gunter. "Dr. Challhert, thank you for being with us tonight."

Gunter nodded and forced and awkward smile, "Thank you for having me."

"Let's just jump right in." She shifted in her seat slightly as she crossed her legs, causing her skirt to ride up a little. "Why do you think the atheist nation experiment is having so many problems?"

Gunter stared a her for a long three seconds as he took a short, measured breath. He swallowed hard.

"Well," he tried to say calmly, "I really don't know. But when I was there, speaking as The Contrarian, I could feel the anger and resentment towards me increase the more I challenged their principles. With each meeting, things got a little more tense."

"Yes, that is quite apparent given the broadcasts during the meetings." She glanced down at her notes then back to him.

"Is it true that you were threatened and that's why you and your wife had to leave?"

She wasted no time getting right to the point which caught him a little off guard. She was staring directly back at him.

How did she know that?

He decided not to gloss over it.

"Yes, Ester, that is true. But that doesn't mean that all of Atheistika is bad. There are always people who resort to violence and think they are doing what is right."

He remembered the blue-eyed man at Brian's house. It caused him to stiffen, but tried not to show it.

"So, you and your wife were forced to flee the Island because of threats due to your views. Is that correct?"

"Well," he said as he gestured with both hands. "I was only carrying out the duties of my office. But some people didn't like how I cross-examined things. Besides they didn't represent Mr. Slarone."

Immediately he remembered the blue-eyed man at Brian's house.

"I see," she said. "And, do you think what you said effected their present situation?"

He paused for another contemplative three

seconds as he leaned back in his chair.

"Ester, to be honest, I'm not really sure. I can only guess."

"Well," she said with a smile, "you're guess would be better than mine."

He returned the smile and glanced past her to Martha who was intently watching him, then back to her.

"Okay," he said with an exhale. "Let me offer something."

He swallowed.

"Without unity, there is chaos. The people of Atheistika are, after all, from all over the world and their values are not entirely homogenous."

He leaned forward just a bit.

"I can only theorize that my challenge of those values uncovered a problem that was already there."

"What problem is that?"

Gunter knew he had to speak his mind so he forced himself to relax as much as possible.

"I would say that when you have a varied collection of people who seek a utopia but don't have unified values or culture, it means there will be problems. Without a solid common moral and cultural base, differences of opinions will abound and dissension arises. Since most people are emotionally connected to their opinions, challenging them means they get emotional. This can lead to resentment, which leads to anger, which in turn leads to problems."

"So, it's an issue of morality, then?"

Another searching glance at Martha, then back. What was he to say? Another swallow.

"Well," he said calmly, "Let me quote from an ancient writer, 'And everyone did what was right in their own eyes.' When that is the case, division, disharmony, and conflict are inevitable."

"I see," she said as she glanced down at her notes.

"So, you think they don't have good morals on Atheistika?"

Gunter realized right away her question was crafted to bring out controversy.

"I did not say that. It's just that different people have different ideas about what is right and wrong. They often base morality on their opinions and feelings. That just doesn't provide a basis for harmony. They'd have to have something bigger than them under which they can all work. Generally, people are pretty good and don't want to hurt others. They just want to live peacefully. You know, that 'do unto others' thing."

"Why then all the riots and violence that are on the increase on the island?"

He stared past her, remembering his time as The Contrarian, hearing the insults, feeling their anger, experiencing the threats. He flexed his jaw muscles and repositioned himself in his chair again. Her examination and his memory of the Island vied for dominance.

He pushed it all away and decided to focus which caused a sense of confidence to well up from within him. He looked at her.

"Let me speak more candidly. We are a flawed race. We think we can lift ourselves up by our bootstraps, solve the world's problems, proclaim what is right and wrong, and gather ourselves in groups of like-minded people. We do this to make ourselves feel secure and good. But, when difficulties arise, what we are really made of becomes evident. The people of Atheistika are no different. They are only showing their true colors as people have done in every culture throughout all of history. All the rules and regulations will not change our desire for self-aggrandizement, comfort, and security. We need something better and bigger than ten truths."

"So, you reject the ten truths?"

"No. Not in principle. It's just that we don't really know if they are true to begin with. I mean, how *can* we know? They are just statements."

"Apparently, your belief seemed to show in how you attacked them back on the island."

Gunter realized her choice of words were meant to elicit yet another reaction. She was prying. Maybe he had already said too much. He considered just bowing out of the interview. But he had said what he had said. What was in him that was motivating him? What was it?

"I didn't attack them. I simply cross-examined them in a manner that was consistent with my office as The Contrarian."

"Yes, you did. Quite well, I might add. Your commentary is being examined and commented on by a lot of people."

"Well, I don't know anything about that. But, like I said, I was just trying to do my job."

She smiled as she looked down at her notes.

He decided to preempt her next question. "In

all my years of experience in teaching philosophy, dealing with people, examining ideas, and teaching my students, I have concluded that we work hard to imitate goodness and truth because we realize it does not naturally dwell within us. We want to improve ourselves because we realize that we need improvement. So, we gather teachers to tickle our ears. We want to be comforted and we want our beliefs verified. But this is ultimately self-centeredness and shortsightedness. And, in the process of acting this out, we have defined our own truths, passed laws to justify our self-gratification, and mocked the traditions of old as though we are superior to our ancestors. This is a dangerous flaw. This is our arrogance. And, I believe it will be our downfall."

He sat back in his chair, surprised by his own words. Had he had spoken the truth? Or, was he only venting? As he waited for the next question, he glanced at a crewmember who was obviously not happy with what he had been saying. He had the same expression of annoyance that he had seen on so many faces on the Island during his times of speaking as The Contrarian.

He looked back at Ester. She had the same expression.

Surprisingly, so did Martha.

ABOUT THE AUTHOR

Matt Slick is a devout Christian who is the founder of carm.org (The Christian Apologetics and Research Ministry) which has had millions of visitors since its inception in 1995. Matt has a live radio show (carm.org/radio) and is the author of several books. He participates in debates, discussions, preaching, teaching, and enjoys promoting the Lord Jesus at every opportunity.

Made in the USA
Lexington, KY
09 October 2018